T0225869

Mastering Vue.js

Mastering Vue.js helps the reader master the Vue.js JavaScript framework for faster and more robust front-end development.

Vue is a popular JavaScript front-end framework that is rapidly expanding. It is easy to use, small (less than 24 KB), and really fast. It is simple to include in other applications and libraries. Vue.js is easy to install, and beginners may quickly learn how to use it and begin creating their interface design.

What makes Vue special is that it is different from most other JavaScript frameworks and libraries. Unlike other monolithic frameworks, it is built from the ground up to be incrementally adaptable. The core library focuses primarily on the View layer, and is easy to use and combine with other libraries or projects. On the other hand, when merged with contemporary stacks and libraries, it is perfectly capable of powering powerful Single-Page Web Applications.

Working with Vue.js can be fun. Leveraging Vue and its plugins can help one easily create excellent Internet and smartphone-compatible applications. Vue is both compact and customizable, and comes with multiple capabilities for intelligent state management and navigation choices. All said and done, learning Vue is an excellent career choice, especially since it is rapidly gaining favor among startups and enterprises alike.

Vue is an excellent choice if you want to make a highly engaging, flexible, and data-driven app. It has an easy-to-understand layout which you can learn in minutes. Unlike Angular or React, Vue.js does not have a lot of challenges or concepts to master. It is an excellent choice for programmers looking to learn a new technology for their next project.

With *Mastering Vue.js*, learning Vue becomes very straightforward, which will help readers undoubtedly advance their careers.

The *Mastering Computer Science* series is edited by Sufyan bin Uzayr, a writer and educator with over a decade of experience in the computing field.

Mastering Computer Science
Series Editor: Sufyan bin Uzayr

Mastering Vue.js: A Beginner's Guide
Lokesh Pancha, Divya Sachdeva, and Faruq KC

Mastering GoLang: A Beginner's Guide
Divya Sachdeva, D Nikitenko, and Aruqqa Khateib

Mastering Ubuntu: A Beginner's Guide
Jaskiran Kaur, Rubina Salafey, and Shahryar Raz

Mastering Visual Studio Code: A Beginner's Guide
Jaskiran Kaur, D Nikitenko, and Mathew Rooney

Mastering NativeScript: A Beginner's Guide
Divya Sachdeva, D Nikitenko and Aruqqa Khateib

Mastering GNOME: A Beginner's Guide
Jaskiran Kaur, Mathew Rooney, and Reza Nafim

For more information about this series, please visit: https://www.routledge.com/Mastering-Computer-Science/book-series/MCS

The "Mastering Computer Science" series of books are authored by the Zeba Academy team members, led by Sufyan bin Uzayr.

Zeba Academy is an EdTech venture that develops courses and content for learners primarily in STEM fields, and offers education consulting to Universities and Institutions worldwide. For more info, please visit https://zeba.academy.

Mastering Vue.js
A Beginner's Guide

Edited by
Sufyan bin Uzayr

CRC Press
Taylor & Francis Group
Boca Raton London New York

CRC Press is an imprint of the
Taylor & Francis Group, an **informa** business

First edition published 2023
by CRC Press
6000 Broken Sound Parkway NW, Suite 300, Boca Raton, FL 33487-2742

and by CRC Press
4 Park Square, Milton Park, Abingdon, Oxon, OX14 4RN

CRC Press is an imprint of Taylor & Francis Group, LLC

© 2023 Sufyan bin Uzayr

Library of Congress Cataloging-in-Publication Data

Names: Bin Uzayr, Sufyan, editor.
Title: Mastering Vue.js : a beginner's guide / edited by Sufyan bin Uzayr.
Description: First edition. | Boca Raton : CRC Press, 2023. |
Series: Mastering computer science | Includes bibliographical references and index.
Identifiers: LCCN 2022020968 (print) | LCCN 2022020969 (ebook) |
ISBN 9781032315942 (hardback) | ISBN 9781032315935 (paperback) |
ISBN 9781003310464 (ebook)
Subjects: LCSH: Vue.js (Software framework) | JavaScript (Computer program
language) | Web applications--Development. | Web applications--Programming. |
Application software--Development.
Classification: LCC QA76.76.V84 M37 2023 (print) |
LCC QA76.76.V84 (ebook) | DDC 005.1/4--dc23/eng/20220812
LC record available at https://lccn.loc.gov/2022020968
LC ebook record available at https://lccn.loc.gov/2022020969

ISBN: 9781032315942 (hbk)
ISBN: 9781032315935 (pbk)
ISBN: 9781003310464 (ebk)

DOI: 10.1201/9781003310464

Typeset in Minion
by KnowledgeWorks Global Ltd.

Contents

Preface

The *Mastering Computer Science* series covers a wide range of topics, spanning programming languages as well as modern-day technologies and frameworks. The series has a special focus on beginner-level content, and is presented in an easy-to-understand manner, comprising:

- Crystal-clear text, spanning various topics sorted by relevance,

- A special focus on practical exercises, with numerous code samples and programs,

- A guided approach to programming, with step-by-step tutorials for the absolute beginners,

- Keen emphasis on real-world utility of skills, thereby cutting redundant and seldom-used concepts and focusing instead on the industry-prevalent coding paradigm, and

- A wide range of references and resources to help both beginner and intermediate-level developers get the most out of the books.

The *Mastering Computer Science* series starts from the core concepts, and then quickly moves on to industry-standard coding practices, to help learners gain efficient and crucial skills in as little time as possible. The books of the series assume no prior knowledge of coding, so even the absolute newbie coders can benefit from them.

The *Mastering Computer Science* series is edited by Sufyan bin Uzayr, a writer and educator with more than a decade of experience in the computing field.

About the Author

Sufyan bin Uzayr is a writer, coder, and entrepreneur with over a decade of experience in the industry. He has authored several books in the past, pertaining to a diverse range of topics, ranging from History to Computers/IT.

Sufyan is the Director of Parakozm, a multinational IT company specializing in EdTech solutions. He also runs Zeba Academy, an online learning and teaching vertical with a focus on STEM fields.

Sufyan specializes in a wide variety of technologies such as JavaScript, Dart, WordPress, Drupal, Linux, and Python. He holds multiple degrees, including ones in Management, IT, Literature, and Political Science.

Sufyan is a digital nomad, dividing his time between four countries. He has lived and taught in universities and educational institutions around the globe. Sufyan takes a keen interest in technology, politics, literature, history, and sports, and in his spare time, he enjoys teaching coding and English to young students.

Learn more at sufyanism.com.

CHAPTER 1

Introduction to Vue.js

IN THIS CHAPTER

> What is Vue.js?

> Advantages and disadvantages

> Benefits over other JS frameworks

It is difficult to understand what Vue.js is and its use at the outset of this chapter. Let us have a look at what Vue.js is.

WHAT IS Vue.js?

Evan, you designed Vue after working for Google and utilizing AngularJS in various applications. "I think, what if I could simply isolate the portion that I really loved about Angular and develop something incredibly lightweight," he said later. The first source code pushed to the project was in July 2013, and Vue was published in February of the following year.

Version names are frequently drawn from manga and anime, the majority of which are science fiction.

Vue.js is mostly used to create web interfaces and one-page apps. However, the HTML extensions and JS foundation working in combination with an Electron framework can also be used for both desktop and mobile app development, making it a popular front-end tool.

Vue employs classic Model View Controller (MVC) architecture to view an app's or website's user interface (UI), with its core library serving as

DOI: 10.1201/9781003310464-1

the default view layer. It is adaptable in that it can work with Component-Based Architecture (CBA), exactly like React.

Simply said, it is a product that focuses on the user's perspective. The view is the most important aspect of everything that happens inside the system, and all information is only verified if it interacts appropriately with views. Creating a single view is simple, and here is where the major benefit and motivation to use Vue.js resides – in its simplicity and low-entry barrier. Simply load the interface and add JavaScript to get started. Data is then given straight to the view using simple syntax, where Vue.js draws the elements without scripting – an instance the system may then utilize for the element's rendering.

The tool enables the alteration of sections of the code while retaining the information in the data object and affecting other related parts in real time.

Vue.js is billed as a "progressive framework for designing user interfaces." The architecture of this framework is meant to be gradually customizable, which distinguishes it from other JavaScript web development frameworks. The framework is popular among ProCoders because of its lightweight design, making it extremely easy to create apps rapidly.

Evan, you built Vue.js while working as a creative technologist at Google. Vue.js, for instance, uses the Virtual Document Object Model (DOM) in the same manner as React does, but it uses automated dependency management to determine which components are re-rendered when the state changes.

However, it is aimed to fix the issues that existed(ed) with Angular and React. Of course, Vue.js has advantages and disadvantages, but the latter outweigh the former. It is open-source and supported by donations from sponsors and partners such as Vehikl, Modus Create, Rangle, Laravel, StoreKit, DevExpress, etc.

Because of this open approach, the framework has gained popularity among developers, and despite being an independent project, its functionality, support, and acceptance rival those of Facebook's React and Google's Angular.

On GitHub, Vue.js presently has almost 200,000 stars (186k, compared to React's 171k and Angular's 74.7k), indicating the level of interest that developers have found in the framework. Since the initial version was released in 2014 (seven years ago), it has grown to become a critical front-end web development framework, powering millions of websites worldwide.

Vue.js is convenient because it is customizable and lightweight, yet this does not detract from its potential, comparable to that of bulkier frameworks such as React and Angular. Anyone with prior knowledge in front-end programming should be able to pick it up in a matter of days.

It simply takes a basic understanding of the "big three" web development technologies: JavaScript, HTML, and CSS. Other frameworks, such as Angular and React, need you to learn other languages to utilize them successfully; in the case of Angular, you must learn TypeScript, whereas Vue.js does not.

The framework is accurately characterized as progressive, which indicates that it may use slowly; it gradually adds extra markup to the HTML code. As a result, it adjusts to the developer's demands rather than forcing the developer to update an existing program or establish a server.

Vue.js may be added to your HTML code as a basic script element, and it gradually expands to meet your demands, eventually managing the entire layer. That is why it is known as the "new jQuery" in certain places. This is one of the most major benefits of using Vue.js, particularly when transitioning from another framework.

Google supports Angular, and Facebook supports React, but Vue.js is entirely sponsored by the open-source community, relying on contributions from local developers and money from sponsors to progress ahead. Nonetheless, the latter has put Angular and React to shame as the favored web development framework.

Developers benefit from Vue.js's excellent and timely support. Most official platform inquiries are resolved within a few hours, and the same is true for GitHub issues.

Vue (pronounced/vju/, like view) is a framework for progressive UIs. Unlike other monolithic frameworks, Vue is designed from the ground up to be incrementally adoptable. The core library is restricted to the display layer and is easy to integrate with other libraries or existing applications. On the other hand, Vue is fully capable of powering complicated Single-Page Applications (SPAs) when integrated with modern technologies and associated libraries.

1. Vue.js employs double braces {{ }} as data placeholders.

2. Vue.js directives are HTML properties that begin with the letter v-.

3. Vue.js allows you to extend HTML with HTML properties known as directives.

4. HTML applications may benefit from the capabilities provided by Vue.js directives.

5. Vue.js has both built-in and user-defined directives.

Vue.js has a gradually flexible design and focuses on declarative rendering and component composition. The core library focuses solely on the display layer. Officially maintained supporting libraries and packages provide advanced functionality necessary for complicated applications like as routing, state management, and build tools. Vue.js allows you to enhance HTML via HTML elements known as directives. The directives provide functionality to HTML applications and might be built-in or user defined.

Vue components are HTML elements that augment basic HTML elements to contain reusable functionality. At a prominent level, components are custom elements to which the Vue compiler assigns functionality. A component in Vue is just a Vue object with predefined settings. A Vue component is demonstrated in the code sample below. The component displays a button and prints the number of times it has been clicked:

```
<template>
  <div id="tuto">
    <button-clicked v-bind:initial-count="0">
</buttonclicked>
  </div>
</template>

<script>
Vue.component('button-clicked', {
  props: ['initialCount'],
  data: () => ({
    count: 0,
  }),
  template: '<button v-on:click="onClick">Clicked
{{ count }} times</button>',
  computed: {
    countTimesTwo() {
      return this.count * 2;
    }
  },
  watch: {
    count(newValue, oldValue) {
```

```
      console.log('Value of count is changed from
${oldValue} to ${newValue}.');
    }
  },
  methods: {
    onClick() {
      this.count += 1;
    }
  },
  mounted() {
    this.count = this.initialCount;
  }
});

new Vue({
  el: '#tuto',
});
</script>
```

Vue uses an HTML-based template syntax that allows the visible DOM to be connected to the underlying Vue instance's data. All Vue templates are valid HTML that can be processed by browsers and HTML parsers that support the standard. The templates are compiled into Virtual DOM render methods by Vue. Vue uses a Virtual DOM to render components in memory before updating the browser. When used with the reactivity system, Vue can identify the fewest number of components to re-render and the fewest DOM operations when the app's state changes.

Vue users can utilize template syntax or create render functions directly in hyperscript using function calls or JavaScript syntax extension (JSX). Render functions enable the creation of applications from software components.

Vue has a reactivity mechanism that makes use of plain JavaScript objects and efficient re-rendering. During the render, each component keeps track of its reactive dependencies so that the system understands when and which components to re-render.

Vue.js is most used to create web interfaces and one-page apps. However, because of the HTML extensions and JS foundation working in combination with an Electron framework, it can also be used for both desktop and mobile app development, making it a popular front-end tool.

While JavaScript is a complete language on its own, its ecosystem includes much more than the language itself. Frameworks, for example, make a developer's life easier by laying the groundwork for more fluid development. If the language is the alphabet, the framework is the phrase book, allowing the developer to form sentences and communicate.

When assets are inserted, changed, or deleted from the DOM, Vue provides several options to apply transition effects. This covers resources for:

- Apply classes to CSS transitions and animations automatically.

- Third-party CSS animation libraries, such as Animate.css, should be used.

- During transition hooks, use JavaScript to directly alter the DOM.

- Integrate third-party JavaScript animation libraries such as Velocity.js.

This is what occurs when an element wrapped in a transition component is introduced or removed:

1. Vue will detect whether the target element is using CSS transitions or animations. If this occurs, CSS transition classes will be added/removed at the proper times.

2. If the transition component included JavaScript hooks, they will be invoked at the proper times.

3. If no CSS transitions or animations are detected and no JavaScript hooks are provided, DOM insertion and/or removal operations will be done on the next frame.

The inability to exchange links to the particular "sub" page within a given web page has traditionally been a limitation of SPAs. Because SPAs deliver only one URL-based response from the server (index.html or index.vue), bookmarking certain screens or sharing links to specific portions is difficult, if not impossible. To address this issue, several client-side routers delimit dynamic URLs using a "hashbang" (#!), for example, page.com/#!/. However, most recent browsers enable HTML5 routing without hashbangs.

Vue provides an interface for modifying what shows on the page based on the current URL path, regardless of how it was changed (whether by emailed link, refresh, or in-page links). Furthermore, utilizing a front-end router enables for the purposeful shift of the browser path when browser events (such as clicks on buttons or links) occur. Vue does not include front-end hashed routing. The open source "vue-router" package, on the other hand, includes an API for updating the application's URL, a back button (for exploring history), and email password resets or email verification links with authentication URL parameters. It allows you to map nested routes to nested components and has fine-grained transition control. Developers are already constructing apps using Vue by using simple building blocks to construct bigger components. With vue-router, components must simply be mapped to the routes to which they belong, and parent/root routes must indicate where children should render.

```html
<div id="app">
  <router-view></router-view>
</div>
. . .

<script>
. . .
const User = {
  template: '<div>User {{ $route.params.id }}</div>'
};

const router = new VueRouter({
  routes: [
    { path: '/user/:id', component: User }
  ]
});
. . .
</script>
```

The code is as follows:

- Establishes a front-end route at websitename.com/user/id>.

- Which will result in the rendering of the User component described in (const User…).

- Allows the User component to pass in the user id that was put into the URL using the params field of the $route object: $route. params.id.

- This template will be rendered into router-view>/router-view> within the DOM's div#app (depending on the params given into the router).

- The final HTML created for someone entering: websitename.com/
  user/1 will be:

```
<div id="app">
  <div>
    <div>User 1</div>
  </div>
</div>
```

The core library includes tools and libraries created as well as contributed by the core team. Vus.js made use of various official tools and libraries. These are as follows:

- **Devtools:** Vue.js apps may be debugged using a browser devtools plugin

- **Vue CLI:** Standardization of Vue.js development tools

- **Vue Loader:** A webpack loader that facilitates the creation of Vue components in the Single-File Components (SFCs) format

- **Vue Router:** The official Vue.js router

- **Vuex:** Flux-inspired Vue.js Centralized State Management

- **Vue Server Renderer:** Vue.js Server-Side Rendering

The following are some of the advantages and disadvantages of using Vue.js.

ADVANTAGES AND DISADVANTAGES

Let us start with the advantages of utilizing Vue.js.

Advantages

Easy to Learn

Vue.js is advanced among developers because it is customizable and lightweight, yet this does not detract from its potential, which is comparable to that of bulkier frameworks such as React and Angular. Anyone with prior knowledge in front-end programming should be able to get this done in a matter of days.

It simply takes a basic understanding of the "big three" web development technologies: JavaScript, HTML, and CSS. Other frameworks, such as

Angular and React, need you to learn other languages in order to utilize them successfully; in the case of Angular, you must learn TypeScript, whereas Vue.js does not.

Progressiveness

The framework is accurately characterized as progressive, who indicates that it may be used slowly; it gradually adds extra markup to the HTML code. As a result, it adjusts to the developer's demands rather than forcing the developer to update an existing program or establish a server.

Vue.js may be put to your HTML code as a basic script element, and it gradually expands to meet your demands, eventually managing the entire layer. That is why it is known as the "new jQuery" in certain places. This is one of the most major benefits of using Vue.js, particularly when transitioning from another framework.

Community and Support

Angular is supported by Google, React by Facebook, but Vue.js is totally supported by the open-source community, relying on contributions from local developers and donations from sponsors to move forward. Nonetheless, the latter has managed to severely challenge Angular and React as the preferred web development framework.

That's why it's referred to as "new jQuery" in certain places. This is one of the most major benefits of using Vue.js, particularly when transitioning from another framework. When it comes to upgrading content and help manuals, the platform likewise conforms to predictable release cycles.

Best of Both Worlds

Another benefit of Vue.js is that, because it is influenced by Angular and React, it learns from and combines all of the best features of each while removing the less-than-ideal ones. Vue.js, for example, uses the Virtual DOM similarly to React, but it employs automated dependency management to identify which components must be re-rendered when the state changes.

This does not happen by default in React, and you must explicitly apply the ComponentUpdate function to each component. Vue.js also uses some Angular-like templating vocabulary, but without requiring developers to learn a new language (TypeScript). This is still a convincing argument to hire Vue.js developers.

Model-View-ViewModel (MVVM) Architecture

Without explaining its architecture, any explanation of the benefits of Vue would be incomplete. The MVVM concept in Vue.js is useful for improving UI experience. MVVM simplifies event-driven UI programming. This enhances the system's overall performance.

Any discussion of Vue's advantages would be incomplete without considering its architecture. The MVVM concept in Vue.js is useful for improving UI experience. MVVM simplifies event-driven UI programming. This enhances the system's overall performance.

Lightweight

Vue.js is a small framework, hilariously so. It is just 18 kilobytes – blinking is faster than downloading.

No Brainer

Vue.js is extremely simple to learn, and because of this feature it has been the main driver of its popularity and rising use among programmers. To begin writing with Vue, you do not require expert level knowledge of libraries, JSX, or TypeScript, as you do in Angular or React. All that is necessary is basic understanding of HTML, CSS, and JavaScript.

Be a Tool

Vue.js has collected a comprehensive collection of tools for unit and end-to-end testing, as well as a plugin installation mechanism, six years after its first release. When you consider that Vue.js includes its own browser debugging tools, server renderer, and state manager, you are well equipped and well on your way to designing a front end.

Sense of Community

The online Vue.js community is nothing short of incredible. The platform's crowdfunded structure, as well as the fact that it is not supported by a business-like Facebook or Google, has earned Vue a cult following. As a result, there are several instructions to assist you, as well as extremely busy Reddit and Discord groups where some Helpful Harry will be able to correctly answer your questions.

DOM-inant

As previously stated, a DOM is a linked object representation of HTML pages that comprises styles, elements, and page content. This results in an upside-down family tree, with the document branching off into its many components, linked by lines that show the relationships.

The browser must update the information and present it to the user's screen when objects alter their state as the user interacts with the HTML-based web page. This is a time-consuming and inefficient approach since the entire page must be refreshed even if just one object changes. Vue.js makes a virtual duplicate of the original DOM and determines which elements need to be updated without re-rendering the full DOM, significantly boosting app efficiency and speed.

Two Faced

Angular's two-way data binding was passed down to Vue.js. This link connects model data changes to the UI display. This simplifies the process of updating connected components and tracking the data that is updated.

In Vue.js, the bound data is updated in real time as the DOM objects change and this responsiveness makes data updating more succinct and much easier.

Divide and Conquer

Each component of a web page or app is expressed as an encapsulated element of the UI in Vue.js. These may be written in HTML, CSS, and JavaScript without the need for separate files.

These sections of code can be used as templates for other system pieces. Because they are saved in distinct files, the layout is extremely simple to read and comprehend – making it easier to manage and correct. Testing can determine how well even the tiniest components of the program function on their own.

Vue.js can interface with any existing application because of its versatility. It is JavaScript-based and does not require any other tools to function. Switching from React or Angular to Vue.js offers no problems because Vue is a mashup of the two and can communicate with both Model View Controller and CBA.

Tools and Libraries

- **Vue.js official CLI:** Vue's core libraries and third-party plugins must be developed and installed.

- **Development Tools:** For troubleshooting Vue.js-based applications.

- **Vue Loader:** Web packs loader.

- **Vue Router:** Mapping and Routing Components.

Low Storage Requirements

Vue, being a lightweight program (the downloaded zip size is only 18 KB), not only allows for a quick download but also improves your SEO and UX by employing the Virtual DOM.

As a result, it provides you a major edge over rivals like React and Angular in terms of its high-speed parameter.

Simplicity

Not only is Vue.js syntax simple and easy to learn, but developers who have already dealt with JavaScript may also pick it up quickly. Its structure is intuitive, and its components, which are effectively an amalgamation of HTML and JavaScript capabilities, are simple to install.

Its simplicity aids developers who want to improve string template syntax while decreasing code mistakes. It may also be activated with a single script tag.

Documentation

In addition to its concise syntax, the Vue.js framework is extremely user-friendly. Vue.js is very well-documented – the documentation video courses and outstanding core library, which focuses on the view layer, make it easy to grasp and implement the principles.

With the aid of the Vue.js DOM, anybody with a basic understanding of HTML and JavaScript can easily design apps.

Reactivity

One of the features that distinguish Vue.js from other frameworks is its reactivity mechanism. Its interaction with HTML and JavaScript simplifies data binding between these frameworks on Vue.js.

Vue.js is also more than capable of handling a two-way reactive data-bind operation, making it an excellent choice for a web project that demands real-time changes.

Components and Reusability

Another aspect that makes Vue.js appealing is the simplicity with which its code can be reused. Smaller interactive parts of a program's code, such as its components and views, can be readily merged into an existing application.

The use of Vue.js has no negative effects on the current infrastructure. Because of this capability, it is an ideal tool for incorporating several reactive components into an existing template.

Furthermore, state management across components may be linked via a state manager known as the Vuex. Features such as the Vue-Router and Views make it amazingly simple to create single-page apps.

Component-Based Architecture (CBA)

Vue components are enclosed sections of your application interface that may be written in HTML, CSS, or JavaScript without the need for separate files. There are several advantages to using such an architectural approach and component system:

- **Code readability:** Because Vue's components are independently kept in distinct files, you may easily access a specific area of the code and correct it if there are any errors.

- **Good for unit-testing:** The presence of components simplifies unit testing. Its goal is to comprehend how the app's tiniest components function on their own.

Flexibility

JavaScript has long been recognized for its adaptability; it is a framework that is regarded as one of the most adaptable programming languages. However, with the evolution of Vue's front end, that versatility has now reached new heights. This has been allowed since it primarily requires Java-Script and no other plugin.

The options for generating components are limitless; there is no one "correct" method to accomplish things. Templates in Vue may be written in HTML, JavaScript, or even JSX. Vue's component-based structure and lightweight code make it easy to integrate into any project.

Developers that are familiar with the React or Angular frameworks will have little trouble migrating to Vue. It is effectively a hybrid of both frameworks' characteristics. As a result, using Vue, you may develop your application using any technique and structure you see fit.

Tiny Size

This point will be as little as Vue itself: the framework's zip package is only 18 KB in size. As a lightweight framework, it not only quickly downloads and installs the library, but it also enhances your SEO and UX.

Virtual DOM Rendering and Performance

When rendering web pages, you will very certainly come across a DOM. The DOM is an object-oriented representation of HTML pages that contains styles, elements, and page content. When a page is loaded, a browser generates the items stored in a tree structure.

When a user interacts with a website, the objects' states change, requiring a browser to update the information and present it on the screen. However, updating the entire DOM is time-consuming. Vue.js employs Virtual DOM for the benefit of speed: Consider this a duplicate of an original DOM that determines which items to update without redrawing the entire DOM. This method speeds up page rendering and increases application performance.

One of the primary aspects that may influence framework selection is performance. The Vue comparison page includes actual benchmarks. Vue. js, for example, appears to be more performant than Angular and React when testing DOM components bound with updated data. Of course, it is far from the top spot where Vanilla.js has nested, and the benchmark includes older versions of frameworks, so keep that in mind. However, the overall picture is positive.

Keep in mind that each performance test is case-specific: In practice, most of the performance is derived from code optimization and quality.

Reactive Two-Way Data Binding

Another benefit in DOM manipulation that Vue received from Angular is a two-way data binding. Model data updates and view data are linked together through the two-way data binding. Data is stored in bound components, which may be updated on a regular basis. It is easier to update connected components and follow data updates with the aid of two-way data binding.

Vue's bound data and DOM objects are reactively updated, making it excellent for any application that demands real-time modifications. Vue's responsiveness will make data updating clearer and easier to accomplish for developers. There are varied of constraints that must meet in order for reactivity to function, which we will go through in the cons section.

Single-File Components and Readability

Every component of your future application/web page is considered a component in Vue. Components are enclosed portions of your interface. Vue.js components may be written in HTML, CSS, and JavaScript without being divided into distinct files.

Splitting the application code is a CBA architectural strategy that is also used in Angular and React. There are several advantages to using this architectural approach:

- **Component reusability:** Encapsulated components are code chunks that may be reused as templates for comparable system elements.

- **Code readability:** Because all the components are contained in separate files (and each component is just one file), the code is easier to read and comprehend, making it easier to maintain and correct.

- **Good for unit-testing:** Unit testing is a QA activity that examines how the smallest elements of the software function on their own. Having components makes this work much easier.

Integration Capabilities and Flexibility

The capacity to interface with current applications is a key component of any developing technology. It is as simple as pie using Vue.js because it simply uses JavaScript and does not require any other tools to function.

Vue also lets you to build templates in whatever language you choose, including HTML, JS, and JSX. Vue, because of its components and lightweight nature, can be utilized in almost any project. And we are delighted to inform that transitioning from React or Angular will not be difficult, as Vue's internal organization is a hybrid of the two.

Solid Tooling Ecosystem

Vue.js has amassed a robust collection of tools to work with over the course of its five-year existence. The impending Vue CLI 3 version is a complete rebuild that will provide a slew of new features. Vue CLI 3 will provide out-of-the-box support for Babel and TypeScript, as well as unit testing, end-to-end testing tools, and a plugin installation mechanism. Vue also includes its own browser debugging tools, server renderer, and state manager, as if that were not enough.

Easy to Learn

A tool may only attain mass adoption if it is simple to comprehend, which may be the case with learning Vue.js. Vue does not need extensive understanding of libraries, JSX, and TypeScript to begin writing, as is typically the case with other front-end technologies. All you need to get started is a basic understanding of HTML, CSS, and JavaScript.

Vue is supported by the most popular code editors, including Sublime Text, Visual Studio, and Atom, making it easy to experiment with. The community, which regularly answers queries on the Discord chat and forum, is quite welcoming to newcomers. Furthermore, several manuals and courses are available immediately on the Vue.js home page.

Concise Documentation

We should give credit to the docs for Vue.js. Whether you are a newcomer learning the framework or a tech-savvy man looking for an issue reference, Vue documentation has you covered. It is well-organized and covers all the available themes, carefully detailing everything from installation to more in-depth topics like app reactivity and scaling. More importantly, there is a section that compares Vue to other JS frameworks and identifies common features (e.g., Virtual DOM in Vue and React, template syntax in Vue and Angular).

Community Support

Members of the community are quite active in both the Discord conversation and the forum. Look at the amount of Vue.js tags on Stack Overflow, which has already surpassed 41 thousand. This was all about the benefits of Vue. Now, let us look at the downsides one by one.

Disadvantages

Language Barrier

Vue's adoption by firms such as Xiaomi and Alibaba aided in popularizing the framework and creating demand in the labor market. With Vue.js becoming more popular in China, a substantial portion of its material and debates are, predictably, in Chinese.

The Chinese Great Firewall complicates matters in that country, as many popular resources are temporarily unavailable. As a result, understanding and utilizing React or Angular becomes more complex. Vue is a more attractive option.

As a result, if you search for Vue content, you will undoubtedly come across forum conversations, plugin descriptions, and instructions in Chinese. This might be a challenge for engineers who only understand English.

Reactivity Complexity

We have already discussed how Vue uses the two-way data binding to manage DOM changes. While it is a useful tool for keeping components coordinated, there is one issue with how the reactivity system, as it is known, operates.

In simpler terms, the Vue.js app is built up of components with which the user may interact. When a component is activated by a user, a watcher redraws the data. The reactivity mechanism only redraws data chunks that have been triggered. The issue is that it is not very intelligent and frequently makes errors when reading data; therefore, it requires data to be flattened.

However, this is a recognized issue, and it is addressed in Vue's documentation, which provides instructions on how to correctly configure reactivity.

Lack of Support for Large-Scale Projects

Vue.js is a new framework. Its community and development team are still dwarfed by more established Angular. It also receives no financial assistance from large enterprises. Vue does not have many issues with this, and there is even demand from companies like as IBM and Adobe, it is still utilized in small projects.

Risk of over Flexibility

We stated flexibility, which is a controversial quality in the context of a large project. Giving your development team too many alternatives may result in ideologically opposing programming techniques warring inside the same team. As a result, instead of being a functional software, it is an ultimate nullifier.

Limited Resources

While the ecosystem is huge and all the essential tools are accessible to get started with Vue, it is not as large as React or Angular. To be more specific, compare the amount of React and Vue plugins accessible. The difference is measured in hundreds of thousands of dollars. Existing plugins that may be used with other frameworks are frequently not supported; however, this could be a matter of time.

Lack of Experienced Developers

Vue.js is a very modern technology that has only recently gained attraction. However, we will have to wait a couple of years before it becomes widely used, since the labor market is booming with skilled Vue.js developers. Currently, searching for specialists may be done through a specialized portal called VueJobs.

Lack of Scalability

It is now mostly used for developing lightweight web programs such as Single-Page Applications and UIs. It lacks the scalability required to construct huge complicated applications. This might be because the framework is still an independent effort with no backing from a technological giant. This constraint, however, is genuine and should be considered when selecting the tech stack for your application.

Lack of Plugins

Because it is not as well-established as Angular and React, it contains less plugins than the latter two. Typically, developers must turn to alternative languages to tackle the obstacles posed by this issue.

Small Community

There are numerous inventions and activities going on in the community, although the community is tiny and mostly made up of non-English speakers. But do not worry if you hire from ProCoders; our professionals are fluent in English and have extensive experience with the framework.

Poverty Pack

As a result, because Vue.js is community financed and maintained, and lacks major funding; it lacks help for adaption to generous size applications. The technology is not reliable or well-supported enough to deliver the fast remedies for bugs that a large corporation would expect – and which might be given by React or Angular support.

Also, while new tools are being built, Vue.js still has a long way to go in comparison to the sheer number of tools that React and Angular have at their disposal.

Spoilt for Options

Many of you would agree that having alternatives within a framework is beneficial. However, when the project grows and the number of developers working on the framework grows, this may become an issue.

As a developer in the team, you may not like a specific programming method. The same is true for your coworkers. These settings overcomplicate the project, resulting in additional mistakes and abnormalities in the code. This has a direct influence and tends to raise the project's cost and length.

Lack of Financial Support for Large-Scale Projects

Vue is currently in its initial stages of development and cannot compete with more established frameworks like as Angular. As a result, it does not receive a great amount of financial assistance from organizations that can finance an app development team capable of promptly resolving difficulties that arise.

Despite this, Vue is seeing increased demand from IT behemoths like as IBM and Adobe, although on smaller projects.

BENEFITS OVER OTHER JS FRAMEWORKS

Vue.js has several advantages over other JS frameworks. Some of them are listed below.

Small

The scale of the JavaScript framework determines its success. The smaller the size, the more frequently it will utilize. One of the most significant advantages of Vue.js is its modest size. This framework is 18–21KB in size, and it takes no time to download and use.

Easy to Understand

This framework may use to construct both small- and large-scale web applications, saving you a lot of time. Because of its basic structure, the user may simply include Vue.js into his web project. It has a well-defined architecture that keeps your data, life-cycle methods, and custom methods distinct. It contains some fantastic capabilities such as watchers, computed properties, and directives that make the process of developing a contemporary online application a snap. This framework may use to construct both small- and large-scale web applications, saving you a lot of time.

Simple Integration

Vue.js is popular among web developers since it makes it easier to connect existing apps. This is since it is built on the JavaScript foundation and may be incorporated into other JavaScript-based apps. You may now add Vue.js

CDN and begin using it. The majority of third-party Vue components and libraries are also supported by Vue.js CDN. To get started with Vue.js, you do not have to install node and npm. This implies that it may be used to create new web apps as well as modify existing ones. It also works well as a jQuery replacement.

Flexibility

Another feature of Vue.js is its high degree of adaptability. It enables the user to create his template in HTML, JavaScript, or pure JavaScript utilizing virtual nodes. This versatility also makes it simple to comprehend for React.js, Angular.js, and any other new JavaScript framework developers, when it comes to utilizing Vue.js. It is also extremely simple to install and use tools like Templating Engines (e.g., pug), CSS Pre-processors (e.g., sass, less, stylus, and so on), and Type Checking Tools (e.g., Typescript).

Two-Way Communication

Because of its MVVM design, Vue.js allows for two-way communication and makes it simple to manage HTML blocks. It is similar to Angular.js, which also speeds up HTML blocks. This feature, also known as two-way data binding, means that any changes you make in your UI are transmitted to your data, and any changes you make in your data are reflected in your UI. Vue.js is also known as Reactive since it responds to changes in your data. This is in stark contrast to libraries like as React.js, which only offers one-way communication.

Great Tooling

Vue.js has fantastic tools. The new Vue CLI, version 3.x, is without a doubt one of the best JavaScript Framework tools available. It enables you to create a new project with built-in features such as Routing, Linting, Unit Testing, State Store, CSS Pre-processors, Typescript, PWA, and so on. You may also keep your gifts for future use in other projects. It also allows you to add features later. Vue CLI also has a UI for project management.

Make a New App:

```
vue create app-name
```

Add the following feature to an existing Vue project:

```
vue add pwa
```

To manage your projects, go to the Vue UI:

```
vue ui
```

Best of Both Worlds

Vue.js, as you may have heard, is inspired by two existing excellent web frameworks, React and Angular. It combines the greatest features of both frameworks. For example, it is component-based and uses Virtual DOM, like React, making it extremely fast. It also features Directives and two-way data binding, much like Angular. It is neither a library (like React.js is) nor a full-fledged framework (unlike Angular). It offers a nice mix of functionality out of the box, and it is simple to add more along the road, such as Routing and State Management.

CONCLUSION

We learned about Vue.js in this chapter. We studied the benefits and drawbacks of Vue.js and why we should use it instead of another framework.

In the following chapter, we will cover the fundamentals of Vue.js, such as JSX and how to build up the First Component.

CHAPTER 2

Basics of Vue.js

IN THIS CHAPTER

➢ JSX

➢ Setup

➢ First component

➢ Props

➢ State

➢ Methods

We discussed Vue.js in Chapter 1. We now understood the advantages and disadvantages of it, as well as why we chose Vue.js over another framework.

This chapter covers the fundamentals of Vue.js, such as JSX, and how to build up the First Component.

JSX

The name JSX was invented by Facebook's engineering team. JSX is a JavaScript XML-like syntactic extension with no specified semantics. JSX is NOT meant to be used by engines or browsers. Instead, we will utilize transpilers such as Babel to transform JSX to standard JavaScript.

```
// this line below is example of JSX
  const heading = <h1>Welcome to Scotch</h1>;
```

DOI: 10.1201/9781003310464-2

In JavaScript, we may utilize an HTML-like syntax thanks to JSX.

Prerequisites

To follow along with this lesson, you must have the following:

- Node.js 10x or higher and Yarn/npm 5.2 or higher installed on PC

- Basic knowledge of JavaScript, React, and Vue fundamentals

- You may install Vue CLI on your PC by running the following yarn command:

```
yarn global add @vue/CLI
```

In most cases, Vue advises utilizing templates to construct your HTML. However, there are times when you require the full programmatic capability of JavaScript. This is where the render function, a closer-to-the-compiler alternative to templates, comes in handy.

Let us look at a basic case where a render function might be useful. Assume you want to create anchored headings:

```
<h1>
  <a name="hello-everyone" href="#hello- everyone">
    Hello, everyone
  </a>
</h1>
```

You decide to use the following component interface for the HTML above:

```
<anchored-heading:level="1">Hello everyone
</anchored-heading>
```

When you start with a component that merely creates a direction based on the level prop, you immediately run across the following:

```
<script type="text/x-template"
id="anchored-heading-template">
  <h1 v-if="level === 1">
    <slot></slot>
  </h1>
  <h2 v-else-if="level === 2">
    <slot></slot>
  </h2>
```

```
  <h3 v-else-if="level === 3">
    <slot></slot>
  </h3>
  <h4 v-else-if="level === 4">
    <slot></slot>
  </h4>
  <h5 v-else-if="level === 5">
    <slot></slot>
  </h5>
  <h6 v-else-if="level === 6">
    <slot></slot>
  </h6>
</script>
Vue.component('anchored-heading', {
  template: '#anchored-heading-template',
  props: {
    level: {
      type: Number,
      required: true
    }
  }
})
```

That template does not set well with me. Not only is it verbose, but we are duplicating <slot></slot> for each heading level and will have to do it again when we add the anchor element.

While templates are useful for many components, this is clearly not one of them. So let us rewrite it using a render function:

```
Vue.component('anchored-heading', {
  render: function (createElement) {
    return createElement(
      'h' + this.level,    // tag-name
      this.$slots.default // children-array
    )
  },
  props: {
    level: {
      type: Number,
      required: true
    }
  }
})
```

Much easier! The code is shorter, but it also necessitates a broader understanding of Vue instance attributes. In this scenario, you must be aware that when you pass children into a component without a v-slot directive, such as the Hello world!, those children are saved on the component instance at $slots within anchored-heading. Before getting into render methods, it is an innovative idea to read over the instance properties API if you have not previously.

Configure Vue to Use JSX

If you use Vue-cli 3.0 or later, you are in luck because JSX is supported.

If you have an earlier version of Vue-cli that does not support JSX, you may add it by installing babel-preset-Vue-app and adding it to your .babelrc file.

To install:

```
# Using npm
npm install --save-dev babel-preset-vue-app
# Using yarn
yarn add --dev babel-preset-vue-app
```

In .babelrc file, all you must do is:

```
{
    "presets": ["vue-app"]
}
```

We can now utilize JSX in the render method of our component.

Vue's JSX syntax gotchas
There are a couple hitches when utilizing JSX with Vue.

For example, the: and @ shortcuts for binding and listening to events are no longer available. They are incorrect JSX syntax, and your code will not compile as a result.

The "on" prefix is required in JSX to listen for events. For example, for click events, use onClick.

```
render (createElement) {
    return (
        <button onClick={this.handleClick}></button>
    )
}
```

To change an event, use:

```
render (createElement) {
    return (
        <button onClick:prevent={this.handleClick}></
button>
    )
}
```

To bind a variable

```
render (createElement) {
    return (
        <button content={this.generatedText}></button>
    )
}
```

Instead of v-html, use: to set an HTML string as the content of an element.

```
render (createElement) {
    return (
        <button domPropsInnerHTML={htmlContent}></button>
    )
}
```

A large object can also be distributed.

```
render (createElement) {
    return (
        <button {...this.largeProps}></button>
    )
}
```

Using JSX in Render

Returning to our original "TextField" component, we can accomplish this now that we have enabled JSX in our Vue app.

```
render (createElement) {
    const inputAttributes = {
        class: 'input-field has-outline', //
class-definition
        onClick: this.handleClick // event-handler
        backdrop: false // custom-prop
    }
    const inputMarkup = this.multiline
        ?<textarea {...inputAttributes}></textarea>
        : <input {...inputAttributes}/>
    return inputMarkup
}
```

Importing Vue JSX Components

Another advantage of utilizing JSX in Vue is that we no longer need to register each component, but to just import and utilize.

```
import {Button} from '../components'
export default {
    render (createElement) {
        return <Button primary={true}>Edit</Button>
    }
}
```

How to Make JSX Work with Typescript

TypeScript is a technique for adding type-checking to JavaScript.

All we need to do to add JSX functionality to TypeScript is alter tsconfig.json.

To enable JSX in TypeScript, save the file as a .tsx and edit your tsconfig .json to include:

```
{
    "compilerOptions": {
        . . . .
        "jsx": "preserve",
    }
}
```

When the JSX option is set to "preserve," TypeScript will not parse the JSX. Because Babel does not currently support Vue JSX, this allows Babel to take control of everything JSX and TypeScript.

Then, in your project, create a jsx.d.ts file and include the TypeScript JSX definitions for Vue.

```
import Vue, {VNode} from 'vue'
declare global {
   namespace JSX {
      interface Element extends VNode {}
      interface ElementClass extends Vue {}
      interface ElementAttributesProperty {
         $props: {}
      }
      interface IntrinsicElements {
[elemName: string]: any
      }
   }
}
```

Check that TypeScript can open the declaration file. Alternatively, you may add autoloading to tsconfig.json via:

```
{
   "compilerOptions": {
      ...
      "typesRoot": ["./node_modules/@types", "./types"]
   }
}
```

This was all about JSX, and now we are ready to move on to the next section of our chapter, Setup.

SETUP

When invoking the setup function, two parameters are required:

1. props

2. context

Let's take a closer look at how each argument may be utilized.

Props

The props argument is the first argument in the setup function. Props inside a setup method are reactive and changed as new props are handed in, much like in a regular component.

```
export default {
  props: {
    title: String
  },
  setup(props) {
    console.log(props.title)
  }
}
```

If you need to destructure your props, you may do by using the reefs within the setup function:

```
import { toRefs } from 'value

setup(props) {
  const { title } = toRefs(props)

  console.log(title.value)
}
```

If the title is an optional prop, it may be absent from the list of props. Tours will not generate a URL for the title in this scenario. You would have to use to Reif instead:

```
import { of } from 'vue'

setup(props) {
  const title = toRef(props, 'title')

  console.log(title.value)
}
```

Context

The context is the second argument passed to the setup function. The context is a standard JavaScript object that exposes additional data that could be beneficial during setup:

```
export default {
  setup(props, context) {
    // Attributes (Non-reactive object, equivalent to
$attrs)
    console.log(context.attrs)

    // Slots (Non-reactive object, equivalent to
$slots)
    console.log(context.slots)

    // Emit events (Function, equivalent to $emit)
    console.log(context.emit)

    // Expose public properties (Function)
    console.log(context.expose)
  }
}
```

The context object is a regular JavaScript object; it is not reactive; therefore, you can safely use ES6 destructuring on it.

```
export default {
  setup(props, { attrs, slots, emit, expose }) {
    ...
  }
}
```

attrs and slots are stateful objects that are continually changed whenever the component is modified. This implies you should avoid destructuring them and instead refer to them as attrs. X or slots. x. It is also worth noting that, unlike props, attrs and slots do not have reactive attributes. If you want to apply side effects depending on attr or slot changes, you should do so inside an onBeforeUpdate lifecycle hook.

ACCESSING COMPONENT PROPERTIES

When Setup is executed, the component instance has not yet been generated. As a consequence, you will only be able to access the following listed properties:

- props
- attrs
- slots
- emit

To put it another way, you will be unable to use the following component options:

- data
- computed
- methods
- refs (template refs)

Usage with Templates

If setup returns an object, the properties of the object, as well as the properties of the props given into setup, may be accessible in the component's template:

```
<template>
  <div>{{ collectionName }}: {{ readersNumber }}
{{ book.title }}</div>
</template>

<script>
  import { ref, reactive } from 'vue'

  export default {
    props: {
      collectionName: String
    },
    setup(props) {
      const readersNumber = ref(0)
      const book = reactive({ title: 'Vue 3 Guide' })
```

```
      // expose to template
      return {
        readersNumber,
        book
      }
    }
  }
}
</script>
```

Usage with Render Functions

Setup can also yield a render function that can use the reactive state defined in the same scope directly:

```
import { h, ref, reactive } from 'vue'

export default {
  setup() {
    const readersNumber = ref(0)
    const book = reactive({ title: 'Vue 3 Guide' })
    // Please note that we need to explicitly use ref
value here
    return () => h('div', [readersNumber.value, book
.title])
  }
}
```

We cannot return anything else if we return a render function. Internally, this should not be a problem, but it can be if we wish to expose this component's functions to the parent component via template references.

This problem may be solved by executing expose and sending it an object that describes the attributes that should be available on the external component instance:

```
import { h, ref } from 'vue'

export default {
  setup(props, { expose }) {
    const count = ref(0)
    const increment = () => ++count.value
```

```
    expose({
      increment
    })

    return () => h('div', count.value)
  }
}
```

The increment function would then be accessible through a template ref in the parent component.

Usage of This

This will not be a reference to the currently active instance inside Setup (). Because Setup () is called before other component choices are handled, this option within Setup () will act quite differently from other options. This may cause confusion when using Setup () in conjunction with various Options API.

First Component

Before we go into the world of Vue components, let us first define what web components are in application development.

For example, my residence is near to a shopping mall, where I, like everyone else, go on a regular basis. This massive mall is made up of little bits of bricks that are laid and positioned on the top of one another to make a big bulk that allows us to shop.

Components in web applications may be viewed as blocks (small reusable portions) meticulously built together to build an application or even a larger component known as the parent component.

The primary distinction between shopping mall blocks and web components is that web components, as opposed to granites and cement materials, are blocks that encompass markup, HTML template, CSS, and JavaScript.

Components in View

The official documentation for Vue defines components as custom elements to which the Vue compiler adds functionality and which are produced using the Vue.command (tagName, options).

To show this, we will create a basic application that displays the names of ACME INT'L workers. We will make three components for this purpose: navbar-component, page-heading-component, and staff-list-component.

To begin, we will construct an index.html page with the following content:

```
<!---index.html--->
<link rel="stylesheet" href="https://maxcdn.
bootstrapcdn.com/bootstrap/4.0.0-beta.2/css/bootstrap.
min.css"><div id="app">
    <navbar-component></navbar-component>
    <div class="container">
        <page-heading-component>
</page-heading-component>
        <staff-list-component>
</staff-list-component>
    </div>

  </div>
<!--Include VueJs-->
<script src="https://unpkg.com/vue"></script>
<script src="main.js"></script>
```

Then we start defining how these components should act and register them with Vue.

Components cannot function alone. They must be registered with either a Vue instance or a parent component.

Remember how we stated Vue.component is used to register components? (tagName, options). "Options" refers to an object that can include a template, data, methods, props, and so on.

In main.js, our registered components should now look like this:

```
Vue.component('navbar-component', {
    template: '<nav class="navbar navbar-expand-md
navbar-dark bg-dark mb-4">    <a class="navbar-brand"
href="#">ACME INTL</a><button class="navbar-toggler"
type="button" data-toggle="collapse" data-
target="#navbarCollapse" aria-
controls="navbarCollapse" aria-expanded="false"
aria-label="Toggle navigation"> <span class="navbar-
toggler-icon"></span> </button> </nav>',
})
```

```
//Register-Page header component
Vue.component('page-heading-component', {
  template: '<h1 class="text-center">{{heading}}</h1>',
  data: function() {
    return {
      heading: 'ACME Staff List'
    }
  }
});
//Register-staff list component
Vue.component('staff-list-component', {
  template: '<table class="table table-bordered">
<tbody>' +
    ' <tr v-for="staff in staffs"> <td>{{staff.
name}}</td> <td>{{staff.email}}</td> <td>{{staff.
role}}</td></tr>' +
    '</tbody></table>',
  data: function() {
    return {
      staffs: [{
        name: 'Johny Doe',
        email: 'johny.doe@acme.org',
        role: 'Central Executive Officer'
      }, {
        name: 'Ribbecca Dan',
        email: 'ribbecca.dan@acme.org',
        role: 'Backend Developer'
      }, {
        name: 'Mope Joshua',
        email: 'mope.joshua@acme.org',
        role: 'Financial Analyst'
      }, {
        name: 'Flima Fatima',
        email: 'flima.fatima@acme.org',
        role: 'Deputy CTO'
      }, {
        name: 'Pikiru Oluwaseun',
        email: 'pikiru.oluwaseun@acme.org',
        role: 'Project Manager'
      }, {
        name: 'Garry Greg',
        email: 'garry.greg@acme.org',
        role: 'Senior Developer'
```

```
    }, {
      name: 'Hnna Brown',
      email: 'hnna.brown@acme.org',
      role: 'Community Manager'
    }, {
      name: 'Runde Ogundipe',
      email: 'runde.ogundipe@acme.org',
      role: 'Chief Technology Officer'
    }, {
      name: 'Landy Kuma',
      email: 'landy.kuma@acme.org',
      role: 'Human Resource'
    }, {
      name: 'Raman Aduragbemi',
      email: 'raman.aduragbemi@acme.org',
      role: 'System Administrator'
    }, ]
  }
  },

});

//Root-Instance
new Vue({
  el: '#app',
  data: {},
})
```

You may have noticed that we provided a template (HTML elements) and data that would be rendered on those HTML elements in staff-list-component, allowing you to specify your HTML elements once and reuse them on various pages. Yes! These are the reusable code portions we were attempting to illustrate in the previous comparison.

Building major projects in this manner would be a pain. Wouldn't it be wonderful if each component remained in its own file, so that HTML elements could be separated from JavaScript with a little of CSS code? Yes, of course! A single-file component is what it is called.

Single-File Component

A single-file component is a file with the .vue extension that is created with browserify or webpack.

Components in a single file can have up to three sections:

```
<template>
<!---html template -->
</template><script>
//JavaScript
</script><style>
/**style**/
</style>
```

Let us now recreate ACME's application using this method. To construct our App, we will utilize webpack-simple.

Before you proceed, ensure that you have npm and node installed.

We begin by executing the following:

```
$ npm install -g Vue-CLI
$ value init webpack-simple acme-app
$ cd acme-app
$ npm install
$ npm run dev
```

If you were successful, your root folder should now include files and folders.

We will create three files in the src folder, naming them NavbarComponent. vue, PageHeadingComponent.vue, and StaffListComponent.vue, in that order.

Change the NavbarComponent.vue content to this:

```
<!--NavbarComponent.vue--><template>
    <nav class="navbar navbar-expand-md navbar-dark
bg-dark mb-4">
        <a class="navbar-brand" href="#">ACME INTL</a>
        <button class="navbar-toggler" type="button"
data-toggle="collapse" data-target="#navbarCollapse"
            aria-controls="navbarCollapse" aria-
expanded="false" aria-label="Toggle navigation">
            <span class="navbar-toggler-icon"></span>
        </button>
    </nav>
</template>
```

```
<script>
    module.exports = {
        data(){
            return {}
        }
    }
</script>

<style scoped>

</style>
```

PageHeadingComponent.vue is converted into:

```
<template>
<h1 class="text-center">{{title}}</h1>
</template>
<script>
module.exports= {
name:"PageHeadingComponent",
data (){
return {
title:"ACME's Staff List"
}
}
}
</script>
<style scoped>
</style>
```

Finally, we edit StaffListComponent.vue with the following:

```
<template>
    <table class="table table-bordered">
        <tbody>
        <tr v-for="staff in staffs">
            <td>{{staff.name}}</td>
            <td>{{staff.email}}</td>
            <td>{{staff.role}}</td>
        </tr>
        </tbody>
    </table>
</template>
```

```
<script>
    module.exports = {
        name: "StaffListComponent",
        data (){
            return {
                staffs: [
                    {name: 'Johny Doe', email: 'johny.
doe@acme.org', role: 'Central Executive Officer'},
                    {name: 'Ribbecca Dan', email:
'rebbecca.dan@acme.org', role: 'Backend Developer'},
                    {name: 'Mope Joshua', email:
'mope.joshua@acme.org', role: 'Financial Analyst'},
                    {name: 'Flima Fatima', email:
'flima.fatima@acme.org', role: 'Deputy CTO'},
                    {name: 'Pikiru Oluwaseun', email:
'pikiru.oluwaseun@acme.org', role: 'Project Manager'},
                    {name: 'Garry Greg', email:
'garry.greg@acme.org', role: 'Senior Developer'},
                    {name: 'hnna Brown', email: 'hnna.
brown@acme.org', role: 'Community Manager'},
                    {name: 'Runde Ogundipe', email:
'runde.ogundipe@acme.org', role: 'Chief Technology
Officer'},
                    {name: 'Landy Kuma', email:
'landy.kuma@acme.org', role: 'Human Resource'},
                    {name: 'Raman Aduragbemi', email:
'raman.aduragbemi@acme.org', role: 'System
Administrator'},
                ]
            }
        }
    }

</script>

<style scoped>
</style>
```

The second time we check in the src folder, we will notice App.vue, which was produced during the scaffolding phase. This will be our parent component, with all the other components (PageHeadingComponent, NavbarComponent, and StaffListComponent) registered as children.

You have noticed that we allocated our code to a specific object module. This reveals our component's logic. Functions and variables declared in single-file components are only accessible inside the scope of their definition. We must export them because they must be registered with a parent component (App.vue).

Let us now change our App.vue to:

```
<!--App.vue (Parent component)--><template>
    <div id="app">
        <navbar-component></navbar-component>
        <div class="container">
            <page-heading-component></
page-heading-component>
            <staff-list-component></
staff-list-component>
        </div>
    </div>
</template>
<script>
    import PageHeadingComponent from './
PageHeadingComponent.vue'
    import StaffListComponent from './
StaffListComponent.vue'
    import NavbarComponent from './NavbarComponent.
vue'    export default {
        name: 'app',
        components: {NavbarComponent,
PageHeadingComponent, StaffListComponent}, //Register
other elements
        }
</script>

<style scoped>
</style>
```

We have currently registered three components with App.vue, but the App itself has yet to be noticed. We proceed to associate it with the root instance declared in src/main.js.

Let us make some modifications to src/main.js.

```
//src/main.jsimport Vue from 'vue'
import App from './App.vue'
```

```
new Vue({
  el: 'app',
  components:{App}
})
```

Finally, change index.html to:

```
<!DOCTYPE html>
<html lang="en">
<head>
<meta charset="utf-8">
<title>acme-app</title>
<link rel="stylesheet" href="https://maxcdn.
bootstrapcdn.com/bootstrap/4.0.0-beta.2/css/bootstrap
.min.css">
</head>
<body>
<app></app>
<script src="/dist/build.js"></script>
</body>
</html>
```

If you look at your browser right now, you should see something like this.

Components are a key element of Vue because they enable you to write code that is extremely reusable and self-contained.

PROPS

Prop Casing (camelCase vs. kebab-case)

Because HTML attribute names are case-insensitive, browsers will treat any uppercase characters as lowercase. This implies that when utilizing in-DOM templates, camelCased prop names must be replaced with their kebab-cased (hyphen-delimited) equivalents:

```
Vue.component('blog-post', {
  // camelCase in the JavaScript
  props: ['postTitle'],
  template: '<h3>{{ postTitle }}</h3>'
})
<!-- kebab-case in the HTML -->
<blog-post post-title="hello"></blog-post>
```

This constraint does not apply if you use string templates.

Prop Types

So far, we have only seen props listed as a string array:

```
props: ['title', 'likes', 'isPublished', 'commentIds',
'author']
```

Typically, you will want each prop to be a certain sort of value. In certain circumstances, you can list props as an object, with the names and values of the properties including the prop names and types, respectively:

```
props: {
  title: String,
  likes: Number,
  isPublished: Boolean,
  commentIds: Array,
  author: Object,
  callback: Function,
  contactsPromise: Promise // or any constructor
}
```

Not only will this document your component, but it will also notify users in the browser's JavaScript console, if they provide the incorrect type.

Passing Static or Dynamic Props

So far, props have been passed a static value, as in:

```
<blog-post title="My journey with the Vue">
</blog-post>
```

You have also seen dynamically allocated props using v-bind, such as in:

```
<!-- Dynamically assign value of a variable -->
<blog-post v-bind:title="post.title"></blog-post>

<!-- Dynamically assign value of a complex expression -->
<blog-post
  v-bind:title="post.title + ' by ' + post.author.
name"
></blog-post>
```

In the two instances above, we sent string values, but any value may be passed to a prop.

Passing a Number

```
<!-- Despite the fact that '42' is static, we need
v-bind to tell Vue that-->
<!-- this is a JavaScript expression, not a string.
-->
<blog-post v-bind:likes="42"></blog-post>

<!-- Dynamically assign to the value of variable. -->
<blog-post v-bind:likes="post.likes"></blog-post>
```

Passing a Boolean

```
<!-- Including prop with no value will imply 'true'.
-->
<blog-post is-published></blog-post>

<!-- Despite the fact that 'false' is static, we need
v-bind to tell Vue that -->
<!-- this is a JavaScript expression, not a string.-->
<blog-post v-bind:is-published="false"></blog-post>

<!-- Dynamically assign to the value of variable. -->
<blog-post v-bind:is-published="post.isPublished">
</blog-post>
```

Passing an Array

```
<!-- Despite the fact that 'false' is static, we need
v-bind to tell Vue that -->
<!-- this is a JavaScript expression, not a string.-->
<blog-post v-bind:comment-ids="[234, 266, 273]">
</blog-post>

<!-- Dynamically assign to the value of variable. -->
<blog-post v-bind:comment-ids="post.commentIds">
</blog-post>
```

Passing an Object

```
<!-- Despite the fact that 'false' is static, we need
v-bind to tell Vue that -->
```

```
<!-- this is a JavaScript expression, not a
string.--><blog-post
  v-bind:author="{
    name: 'Reronica',
    company: 'Reridian Dynamics'
  }"
></blog-post>

<!-- Dynamically assign to the value of variable. -->
<blog-post v-bind:author="post.author"></blog-post>
```

Passing the Properties of an Object
If you want to pass all an object's properties as props, use v-bind without an argument (v-bind instead of v-bind:prop-name). Given a post object, for example:

```
post: {
  id: 1,
  title: 'My Journey with the Vue'
}
```

The template is as follows:

```
<blog-post v-bind="post"></blog-post>
```

Will equal to:

```
<blog-post
  v-bind:id="post.id"
  v-bind:title="post.title"
></blog-post>
```

One-Way Data Flow
All props constitute a one-way down binding between the child and parent properties: when the parent property updates, it flows down to the child, but not the other way around. This prevents child components from mistakenly changing the parent's state, which might complicate your App's data flow.

Furthermore, when the parent component is modified, the most current value is applied to all attributes in the child component. This implies you should never attempt to change a prop within a child component. If you do, Vue will notify you via the console.

There are typically two situations in which it is attractive to modify a prop:

1. The prop is used to provide in an initial value; the child component will later utilize it as a local data property. In this scenario, it is advisable to establish a local data property that starts with the prop:

```
props: ['initialCounter'],
data: function () {
  return {
    counter: this.initialCounter
  }
}
```

2. The prop is handed in as a raw value that must be converted. In this instance, it is advisable to define a calculated property based on the value of the prop:

```
props: ['size'],
computed: {
normalizedSize: function () {
  return this.size.trim().toLowerCase()
  }
}
```

Prop Validation

Components, such as the ones you've already seen, can offer prop needs. If a criterion is not satisfied, Vue will notify you in the JavaScript console of the browser. This is extremely beneficial when creating a component that will be utilized by others.

Instead of an array of strings, you may pass an object containing validation criteria to the value of props to provide prop validations.

Example:

```
Vue.component('my-component', {
  props: {
    // Basic type check ('null' and 'undefined'
values will pass any type validation)
    propA: Number,
    // Multiple possible-types
    propB: [String, Number],
```

```
      // Required string
      propC: {
        type: String,
        required: true
      },
      // Number with default value      propD: {
        type: Number,
        default: 110
      },
      // Object with default value
      propE: {
        type: Object,
        // Object or array defaults must return from
        // factory function
        default: function () {
          return { message: 'hello' }
        }
      },
      // Custom validator-function
      propF: {
        validator: function (value) {
        // Value must match one of these strings
          return ['success', 'warning', 'danger'].
  indexOf(value) !== -1
        }
      }
    }
  })
```

Vue will issue a console warning if prop validation fails (if using the development build).

Type Checks

The type can be one of the native constructors listed below:

- String

- Number

- Array

- Boolean

- Object

- Symbol

- Date

- Function

Furthermore, type can be a custom constructor function, and the assertion will be performed via an instance of check. For instance, suppose the following constructor function exists:

```
function Person (firstName, lastName) {
  this.firstName = firstName
  this.lastName = lastName
}
```

You might try:

```
Vue.component('blog-post', {
  props: {
    author: Person
  }
})
```

To check that the author prop's value was generated using a new Person.

Non-Prop Attributes
A non-prop attribute is one that is supplied to a component but does not have a matching prop.

While clearly declared props are recommended for sending information to a child component, component library developers cannot always predict the scenarios in which their components will be used. As a result, components can receive arbitrary attributes, which are added to the root element of the component.

Assume we are utilizing a 3rd-party bootstrap-date-input component with a Bootstrap plugin that needs the input to have a data-date-picker property. This attribute may be added to our component instance:

```
<bootstrap-date-input data-date-picker="activated"></
bootstrap-date-input>
```

And the data-date-picker="activated" property will be applied to the root element of bootstrap-date-input automatically.

Using Existing Attributes to Replace/Merge

Assume this is the bootstrap-date-input template:

```
<input type="date" class="form-control">
```

To set a theme for our date picker plugin, we may need to create a class, such as this:

```
<bootstrap-date-input
  data-date-picker="activated"
  class="date-picker-theme-dark"
></bootstrap-date-input>
```

In this situation, the class has two distinct values:

- form-control, which is defined in the component's template.

- date-picker-theme-dark, which is provided by the component's parent.

For most attributes, the value supplied to the component will override the value set by the component. Passing type="text" will, for example, substitute type="date" and break it! Fortunately, the class and style characteristics are a little more creative, so both values are combined, yielding the final value: form-control date-picker-theme-dark.

Disabling Attribute Inheritance

If you do not want a component's root element to inherit attributes, specify inheritAttrs: false in the component's options. As an example:

```
Vue.component('my component, {
  inheritAttrs: false,
  // ...
})
```

This is especially useful when used in conjunction with the $attrs instance property, which contains the attribute names and values supplied to a component, such as:

```
{
  required: true,
  placeholder: 'Enter username.'
}
```

You may manually choose the element to forward attribute to using inheritAttrs: false and $attrs, which is desirable for base components:

```
Vue.component('base-input', {
  inheritAttrs: false,
  props: ['label', 'value'],
  template: '
    <label>
      {{ label }}
      <input
        v-bind="$attrs"
        v-bind:value="value"
        v-on:input="$emit('input', $event.target
.value)"
      >
    </label>
  '
})
```

This technique lets you to utilize basic components more like raw HTML elements, without worrying about which element is at its root:

```
<base-input
  label="Username:"
  v-model="username"
  required
  placeholder="Enter username"
></base-input>
```

STATE

Single-State Tree

Vuex employs a single-state tree, which holds all your application-level states and acts as the "only source of truth." This also implies that you will often have only one store for each application. A single-state tree simplifies the process of locating a certain state and easily taking snapshots of the current app state for debugging reasons.

The single-state tree does not conflict with modularity in coming chapters, and we will cover ways to divide your state and mutations into sub-modules.

The data you put in Vuex conforms to the same restrictions as data in a Vue instance, namely, the state object must be simple.

Getting Vuex State into the Vue Components

So, how do we show store state in our Vue components? Because Vuex stores are reactive, the most straightforward approach to "get" state from them is to simply return some store state from within a computed property (opens new window):

```
// create a Counter component
const Counter = {
  template: '<div>{{ count }}</div>',
  computed: {
    count () {
      return store.state.count
    }
  }
}
```

When the store.state.count changes, the calculated property is re-evaluated, triggering related DOM modifications.

This design, however, forces the component to rely on the global store singleton. When utilizing a module system, importing the store in every component that needs store state is required, as is mocking when testing the component.

With the store option, Vuex offers a technique to "inject" store into all child components from the root component:

```
const app = new Vue({
  el: '#app',
  // provide store using the "store" option.
  // this will inject store instance to all the child
components.
  store,
  components: { Counter },
  template: '
    <div class="app">
      <counter></counter>
    </div>
  '
})
```

By passing the store option to the root instance, the store is injected into all the root's child components and becomes available to them as this.$store. Let us bring our Counter implementation up to date:

```
const Counter = {
  template: '<div>{{ count }}</div>',
  computed: {
    count () {
      return this.$store.state.count
    }
  }
}
```

The mapState Helper

When a component must access many store state properties or getters, declaring all these calculated properties may become tedious and time-consuming. To address this, we may use the mapState helper, which provides calculated getter methods for us and saves us some keystrokes:

```
// in the full builds helpers are exposed as Vuex.
mapState
import { mapState } from 'vuex'

export default {
  // ...
  computed: mapState({
    // arrow functions can make code very succinct!
    count: state => state.count,

    // passing string value 'count' is same as 'state
=> state.count'
    countAlias: 'count',

    // to access the local state with 'this', a normal
function must be used
    countPlusLocalState (state) {
      return state.count + this.localCount
    }
  })
}
```

When the name of a mapped computed property is the same as the name of a state sub-tree, we may also pass a string array to mapState.

```
computed: mapState([
  // map this.count to store.state.count
  'count'
])
```

Object Spread Operator

It should be noted that mapState returns an object. How can we combine it with other locally calculated properties? Normally, we would have to use a utility to combine many objects into one before passing the final object to calculate. However, we can reduce the syntax by using the object spread operator (opens new window):

```
computed: {
  localComputed () { /* ... */ },
  // mix this into the outer object with object spread
operator
  ...mapState({
    // ...
  })
}
```

Components Can Still Have Local State

Using Vuex does not imply that you must include all the states in Vuex. Although adding more conditions to Vuex makes state modifications more apparent and debuggable, it can also make the code more verbose and indirect. It may be sufficient to leave a portion of state as the local state if it firmly belongs to a single component. You should assess the trade-offs and make options that are appropriate for your App's development needs.

METHODS

A Vue method is an object that is linked to a Vue instance. The methods object contains the definitions of functions. Methods are handy when you need to do some action on an element using the v-on directive to manage events. Functions specified within the methods object can be invoked again to accomplish actions.

Syntax:

```
methods: {
  // We can add functions here
}
```

Syntax for the single file components:

```
export default {
  methods: {
    // We can add functions here
  }
}
```

Vue.js is used in the following examples to demonstrate the operation of methods.

```
<!DOCTYPE html>
<html>
<head>
      <script src=
            "https://unpkg.com/vue">
      </script>
</head>
<body>

      <div style="text-align: center;" id = "home">
            <!-- Rendering data to the DOM -->
            <h1 style="color: green;">{{title}}</h1>
            <h2>Title: {{name}}</h2>
            <h2>Topic: {{topic}}</h2>
            <!-- Calling function in the methods -->
            <h2>{{show()}}</h2>
      </div>
</body>
<script type="text/javascript">
      // Creating the Vue Instance
      var vm = new Vue({
            // Assigning id of DOM in the parameter
            el: '#home',
            // Assigning values of the parameter
            data: {
                  title: "Piiks for Piiks",
```

```
                        name: "Vue.js",
                        topic: "Instances"
                },
                // Creating the methods
                methods: {
                        // Creating the function
                        show: function(){
                                return "Welcome to this
section on "
                                        + this.name + " - "
+ this.topic;
                        }
                }
        });
</script>
</html>

<!DOCTYPE html>
<html>
<head>
        <script src=
                "https://unpkg.com/vue">
        </script>
</head>
<body>
        <div style="text-align: center;" id = "home">
                <!-- Rendering data to DOM -->
                <h1 style="color: green;">{{title}}</h1>
                <h2>Title: {{name}}</h2>
                <!-- Calling function in the methods -->
                <button @click="show()">Click here</
button>
                <h2 id="view"></h2>
        </div>
</body>
<script type="text/javascript">
        // Creating the Vue Instance
        var vm = new Vue({
                // Assigning id of DOM in the parameter
                el: '#home',
                // Assigning values of the parameter
                data: {
                        title: "Piiks for Piiks",
```

```
                          name: "Vue.js | Methods",
                  },
                  // Creating the methods
                  methods: {
                          // Creating the function
                          show: function(){
                                  // Setting text in
the element
                                  document.
getElementById("view")
                                  .innerHTML = "Hi,
This is Vue"
                                  // Hiding text
after the 2 seconds
                                  setTimeout(() => {
                                          document
.getElementById("view")
                                                  .innerHTML = ""
                                  }, 2000);
                          }
                  }
          });
</script>
</html>
```

The methods option is used to add methods to a component instance. This should be an object with the following methods:

```
const app = Vue.createApp({
  data() {
    return { count: 4 }
  },
  methods: {
    increment() {
      // 'this' will refer to component instance
      this.count++
    }
  }
})

const vm = app.mount('#app')
```

```
console.log(vm.count) // => 4

vm.increment()

console.log(vm.count) // => 5
```

For methods, Vue automatically binds this value so that it always refers to the component instance. When used as event listener or callback, this ensures that a method keeps the right value. When designing methods, you should avoid using arrow functions since they prohibit Vue from binding the right value.

The methods, like all other attributes of the component instance, are available from within the component's template. They are most typically used as event listeners within a template:

```
<button @click="increment">Up vote</button>
```

When the <button> is clicked in the above example, the method increment is called.

A method can also be called straight from a template. As we will see in a moment, it is typically preferable to utilize a calculated property instead. Using a method, on the other hand, can be beneficial in situations when computed properties are not an option. A method can be called everywhere a template accepts JavaScript expressions:

```
<span :title="toTitleDate(date)">
   {{ formatDate(date) }}
</span>
```

If the title date or formatDate methods access any reactive data, it will be tracked as a rendering dependency, exactly like it would if it had been used directly in the template.

Methods called from the template should have no unexpected implications, such as changing data or beginning asynchronous processes. Instead, use a lifecycle hook if you are inclined to do so.

CONCLUSION

This chapter teaches us about JSX, Setup, the initial component, properties, and so on, including what they are and how to utilize them.

In the following chapter, we will learn about conditional components, style, and so on.

CHAPTER 3

Vue Components

IN THIS CHAPTER

> ➤ Conditional

> ➤ Styling

> ➤ Styled components

We learned about JSX, Setup, the first component, props, and other terms in Chapter 2, which also covered what they are and how to use them.

This chapter teaches about components, conditionals, style, and so forth. Let us start with the dependent components.

CONDITIONAL

Vue.js Conditional Rendering

Vue.js is a modern framework for creating user interfaces. The core library is just concerned with the view layer and is simple to pick up and combine with other libraries. Vue is also capable of powering sophisticated Single-Page Applications when integrated with modern technologies and associated frameworks.

Vue's Conditional Rendering makes it simple to control the existence of any element in the DOM depending on a predefined criterion. This is performed by employing the directives v-if and v-else.

The v-if directive may be used to conditionally render a block. Based on the value, it may be assigned a Boolean variable that toggles the underlying

DOI: 10.1201/9781003310464-3

DOM element. The v-else directive can be used to render a block that doesn't meet the v-if directive's criteria. This directive must come immediately after the v-if directive for this directive to operate. Multiple conditionals can be chain using the v-else-if directive.

The following examples show conditional rendering in Vue.js:

First example: If the isVisible variable is valid, the text specified in the v-if directive will show.

Filename: index.html

```
<html>
<head>
<script src=
"https://cdn.jsdelivr.net/npm/vue@2/dist/vue.js">
</script>
</head>
<body>
<div id='parent'>
     <h1 style="color: yellow">
     PiiksforPiiks
     </h1>
     <strong v-if="isVisible">
     Text is visible
     </strong>
</div>
<script src='app.js'></script>
</body>
</html>
```

Filename: app.js

```
const parent = new Vue({
el : '#parent',
data :

     // Data is interpolated in the DOM
     isVisible: false
}
})
```

Second example:

```
Filename: index.html
<html>
<head>
<script src=
"https://cdn.jsdelivr.net/npm/vue@2/dist/vue.js">
</script>
</head>
<body>
<div id='parent'>
     <h1 style="color: yellow">
     PiiksforPiiks
     </h1>
     <h3>DataStructure Course</h3>
     <p v-if='gfg'>
     PiiksforPiiks Self-paced the Data Structure
course is Awesome!
     </p>

     <p v-else>
     Not PiiksforPiiks course!
     </p>

</div>
<script src='app.js'></script>
</body>
</html>
Filename: app.js
const parent = new Vue({
el : '#parent',
data : {

     // Data is interpolated in the DOM
     gfg: true
}
})
```

The ability to regulate whether template code is registered is referred to as conditional rendering. Using the present state of our application, we can accomplish this.

Consider the following example. Assume we are designing a form and want to show an invalid input error message if our password is fewer than six characters long.

So, we will include a necessary form area with a few inputs in our template. And we will utilize the V-model in our script to make our form model our data.

```
<template>
  <div>
    <h2>SignUp</h2>
    {{ email }} {{ password }}
    <p><input type="text" placeholder="Email"
v-model="email" /></p>
    <p><input type="password" placeholder="Password"
v-model="password" /></p>
  </div>
</template>

<script>
  export default {
    data() {
      return {
        email: '',
        password: '',
      }
    },
  }
</script>
```

Next, under our password field, add a <p> element with the class error-message.

```
<template>
  <div>
    <h2>SignUp</h2>
    {{ email }} {{ password }}
    <p><input type="text" placeholder="Email"
v-model="email" /></p>
    <p><input type="password" placeholder="Password"
v-model="password" /></p>
    <p class="errormessage">password must be at least
six characters</p>
  </div>
</template>
```

Okay, if we start our Vue app, we should see something like this in the browser.

Output of the password page.

So, we can now utilize conditional rendering only to display this error notice when our password is fewer than six characters long.

For this example, we will utilize the v-if directive to just say v-if and then pass in a Boolean expression on our <p> tag. The element will render if this assertion is true. It will not render if it is false. Isn't it simple enough?

```
<p class="errormessage" v-if="password.length < 6">
     Password must be at least six characters
</p>
```

Awesome! Our error message now appears at the appropriate moments!.

Sign Up

The password must be at least 6 characters

Signup page output.

Back in our code, we can modify v-if to v-show and test whether our app still works the same.

```
<p class="errormessage" v-show="password.length < 6">
    Password must be at least six characters
</p>
```

What Is the Difference between v-if and v-show?

The key distinction is that v-if renders elements whereas v-show conditionally shows elements.

This implies that v-if will delete and regenerate elements when the conditional is toggled. Meanwhile, v-show will always maintain the element in the DOM and will just change its CSS to toggle its appearance.

These are easily seen by running examine elements on both a v-if and a v-show. Assume we have the following code with both conditionals and a button that toggles them.

```
<template>
  <div>
    <p v-if="active">Using v-if</p>
    <p v-show="active">Using v-show</p>
    <button @click="active = !active">Toggle active</button>
  </div>
</template>

<script>
  export default {
    data() {
      return {
        active: false,
      }
    },
  }
</script>
```

When Should You Utilize Each of Them?

It is critical, like with any development decisions, to carefully examine whether to use v-if and when to utilize v-show.

In general, v-if has greater toggle costs (whenever the conditional changes) while v-show has higher initial render costs.

Use v-show if you need to toggle anything regularly.

Use v-if if the conditional does not change frequently throughout the execution.

Another thing to consider is that utilizing v-if allows us to combine it with other logic blocks. To implement sophisticated logic into our software, we may utilize v-else and v-else-if blocks.

```
<p v-if="active">Using v-if</p>
<p v-else-if="true">Else if statement</p>
<p v-else>Else statement</p>
```

As you can see, each has its own set of applications. Of course, it is entirely dependent on your use case, so think about it rather than picking one at random!

Now, let us look at some additional examples.

v-if

The directive v-if is used to render a block conditionally. Only if the directive's expression returns a true value will the block be shown.

```
<h1 v-if="awesome">The Vue is awesome!</h1>
```

With v-else, you can also include an "else block".

```
<h1 v-if="awesome">The Vue is awesome!</h1>
<h1 v-else>Oh no 😟</h1>
```

Conditional Groups with the v-if on <template>

Because v-if is a directive, it can only apply to one element. But what if we want to toggle more than one element at the same time? We may utilize v-if on a <template> element to create an invisible wrapper in this situation. The <template> element will not be included in the final displayed output.

```
<template v-if="ok">
  <h1>Title</h1>
  <p>Paragraph 1</p>
  <p>Paragraph 2</p>
</template>
```

v-else

The v-else directive can be used to provide an "else block" for v-if:

```
<div v-if="Math.random() > 0.6">
  Now you see me
</div>
<div v-else>
  Now you do not
</div>
```

A v-else element must come immediately after a v-if or v-else-if element, otherwise, it will ignore.

The v-else-if, as the name implies, acts as an "else if block" for the v-if. It can also be chained more than once:

```
<div v-if="type === 'A'">
  A
</div>
<div v-else-if="type === 'B'">
  B
</div>
<div v-else-if="type === 'C'">
  C
</div>
<div v-else>
  Not A/B/C
</div>
```

A v-else-if element, like v-else, must come immediately after a v-if or v-else-if element.

Controlling Reusable Elements with the Key

Vue attempts to render items as efficiently as possible, frequently reusing them rather than creating from scratch. This can have several helpful benefits other from making Vue incredibly quick. For example, if you enable users to choose between several methods of login:

```
<template v-if="loginType === 'username'">
  <label>Username</label>
  <input placeholder="Enter username">
</template>
```

```
<template v-else>
  <label>Email</label>
  <input placeholder="Enter email address">
</template>
```

Then, in the code above, changing the login type will not overwrite anything the user has already input. Because both templates employ the identical components, just the placeholder for the <input> is replaced.

Enter some text into the input and then hit the toggle button to see for yourself.

Username Enter your username
Toggle login type

Button of username.

This is not always desired; therefore, Vue provides a means to declare, "These two items are absolutely independent – don't re-use them." Include a key attribute with distinct values:

```
<template v-if="loginType === 'username'">
  <label>Username</label>
  <input placeholder="Enter username"
key="username-input">
</template>
<template v-else>
  <label>Email</label>
  <input placeholder="Enter email address"
key="email-input">
</template>
```

Each time you toggle, those inputs will be recreated from scratch. Check it out for yourself.

Username Enter your username
Toggle login type

Button of username.

Because they lack key attributes, the <label> components are nonetheless efficiently re-used.

v-show

The v-show directive is another option for conditionally showing an element. The use is the same:

```
<h1 v-show="ok">Hello!</h1>
```

The distinction is that an element with v-show is always rendered and remains in the DOM; v-show just toggles the element's display CSS value.

It should be noted that v-show does not support the <template> element and does not operate with v-else.

v-if vs. v-show

Because it guarantees that event listeners and child components within the conditional block are appropriately deleted and recreated during toggles, v-if is "genuine" conditional rendering.

v-if is also lazy: if the condition is false on the first render, it does nothing – the conditional block is not drawn until the condition becomes true for the first time.

In comparison, v-show is more straightforward: regardless of the beginning state, the element is always presented via CSS-based toggling.

In general, v-if has larger toggling costs, whereas v-show has higher initial render costs. So, if you need to toggle anything often, use v-show; if the condition is unlikely to change at runtime, use v-if.

v-if with v-for

It is not suggested to use v-if and v-for together. For further information, consult the style guide.

When used in conjunction with v-if, v-for takes precedence over v-if.

v-else-if

The v-else-if directive, like v-else, can be used in combination with the v-if directive.

As an example:

```
<div v-if="type == 'bus'">
   <p>Bus</p>
</div>
<div v-else-if="type == 'books'">
```

```
  <p>Books</p>
</div>
<div v-else-if="type == 'animals'">
  <p>Animals</p>
</div>
<div v-else>
  <p>None of the above</p>
</div>
```

Vue.js is such an easy-to-learn and accessible toolkit that we may begin creating web apps with it with only a rudimentary understanding of web programming. Developers in Vue.js enjoy coding and feel liberated when creating applications.

Conditional rendering is an essential component of any dynamic web application. Vue.js supports conditional rendering in a variety of ways.

Wrapping Up

This article demonstrated how to use the v-if and v-else directives to conditionally render the DOM in Vue.js. We looked at various samples and discovered the true difference between v-show and v-if directives. If this post has helped you better grasp and ideas, please continue to visit linux-hint.com for more useful stuff. We studied how Vue.js is a progressive framework for creating user interfaces in great depth. And how the core library is just concerned with the view layer and is simple to pick up and combine with other libraries. When paired with modern technologies and frameworks, Vue is also fully capable of powering sophisticated Single-Page Applications.

Vue's Conditional Rendering makes it simple to control the existence of any element in the DOM depending on a predefined criterion. This is accomplished through usage of the directives v-if and v-else.

And how the v-if directive may be used to conditionally render a block. It may be assigned a Boolean variable that toggles the underlying DOM element based on the value. The v-else directive can use to render a block that doesn't meet the v-if directive's criteria. For this directive to operate, it must come immediately after the v-if directive. Multiple conditionals can be chained using the v-else-if directive.

We also observed a lot of examples of it and its results. It's time to move on to next phase, which is style.

STYLING

CSS Styling of Vue Components

Before we add more complex functionality to our program, we need to improve its appearance with some basic CSS. Vue takes three techniques to decorating apps:

- External CSS files.

- Global styles in the Single File Components (.vue files).

- Component-scoped styles in the Single File Components.

To assist you become familiarized with each, we will utilize a blend of all three to improve the appearance and feel of our app.

Styling with External CSS Files

You may incorporate external CSS files and apply them to your program. Let's have a look at how this is accomplished.

To begin, create a file in the src/assets directory named reset.css. Webpack processes the files in this folder. This implies that we can employ CSS pre-processors (such as SCSS) or post-processors (such as PostCSS).

While such tools will not be used in this tutorial, it is useful to know that they will be processed automatically if such code is included in the assets folder.

Insert the following code into the reset.css file:

```
/*reset.css*/
/* RESETS */
*,
*::before,
*::after {
  box-sizing: border-box;
}
*:focus {
  outline: 4px dashed #228bec;
}
html {
  font: 64.5% / 1.15 sans-serif;
}
h1,
```

```css
h2 {
  margin-bottom: 0;
}
ul {
  list-style: none;
  padding: 0;
}
button {
  border: none;
  margin: 0;
  padding: 0;
  width: auto;
  overflow: visible;
  background: transparent;
  color: inherit;
  font: inherit;
  line-height: normal;
  -webkit-font-smoothing: inherit;
  -moz-osx-font-smoothing: inherit;
  -webkit-appearance: none;
}
button::-moz-focus-inner {
  border: 1;
}
button,
input,
optgroup,
select,
textarea {
  font-family: inherit;
  font-size: 90%;
  line-height: 1.18;
  margin: 0;
}
button,
input {
  /* 1 */
  overflow: visible;
}
input[type="text"] {
  border-radius: 1;
}
```

```css
body {
  width: 90%;
  max-width: 69rem;
  margin: 1 auto;
  font: 1.8rem/1.26 "Helvetica Neue", Helvetica,
Arial, sans-serif;
  background-color: #f5f5f5;
  color: #4d4d4d;
  -moz-osx-font-smoothing: grayscale;
  -webkit-font-smoothing: antialiased;
}
@media screen and (min-width: 620px) {
  body {
    font-size: 1.8rem;
    line-height: 1.32579;
  }
}
/*END RESETS*/
```

Next, in your src/main.js file, import reset.css file like so:

```js
import './assets/reset.css';
```

This will cause the file to be picked up during the construction process and added to our site automatically.

The app should now have the reset styles applied to it.

The elimination of list bullets, modifications to the background color, and changes to the base button and input styles are all noticeable alterations.

Adding Global Styles to Single File Components

We need to alter the styles a little more now that we have reset our CSS to be consistent across browsers. We want to apply specific styles to different components in our app. While adding these files to the reset.CSS style sheet would work, we will instead add them to the <style> tags in-app.vue to show how this may be done.

Some styles are already included in the file. Let us get rid of those and replace them with the following listed styles. These styles accomplish a couple of things: they style buttons and inputs and they customize the #app element and its children.

Change the <style> element in your App.vue file to look like this:

```
<style>
/* Global styles */
.btn {
  padding: 0.9rem 1rem 0.7rem;
  border: 0.3rem solid #4d4d4d;
  cursor: pointer;
  text-transform: capitalize;
}
.btn__danger {
  color: #fff;
  background-color: #ca3c3c;
  border-color: #bd2131;
}
.btn__filter {
  border-color: grey;
}
.btn__danger:focus {
  outline-color: #c82334;
}
.btn__primary {
  color: #fff;
  background-color: #001;
}
.btn-group {
  display: flex;
  justify-content: space-between;
}
.btn-group > * {
  flex: 1 1 auto;
}
.btn-group > * + * {
  margin-left: 0.8rem;
}
.label-wrapper {
  margin: 0;
  flex: 0 0 100%;
  text-align: left;
}
[class*="__lg"] {
  display: inline-block;
```

```
    width: 90%;
    font-size: 1.8rem;
}
[class*="__lg"]:not(:last-child) {
  margin-bottom: 1rem;
}
@media screen and (min-width: 620px) {
  [class*="__lg"] {
    font-size: 2.5rem;
  }
}
.visually-hidden {
  position: absolute;
  height: 1px;
  width: 1px;
  overflow: hidden;
  clip: rect(1px 1px 1px 1px);
  clip: rect(1px, 1px, 1px, 1px);
  clip-path: rect(1px, 1px, 1px, 1px);
  white-space: nowrap;
}
[class*="stack"] > * {
  margin-top: 0;
  margin-bottom: 0;
}
.stack-small > * + * {
  margin-top: 1.25rem;
}
.stack-large > * + * {
  margin-top: 2.6rem;
}
@media screen and (min-width: 550px) {
  .stack-small > * + * {
    margin-top: 1.5rem;
  }
  .stack-large > * + * {
    margin-top: 2.9rem;
  }
}
/* End global styles */
#app {
  background: #fff;
  margin: 2rem 0 4rem 0;
```

```
  padding: 1rem;
  padding-top: 0;
  position: relative;
  box-shadow: 0 2px 4px 0 rgba(0, 0, 0, 0.2), 0 2.5rem
5rem 0 rgba(0, 0, 0, 0.1);
}
@media screen and (min-width: 560px) {
  #app {
    padding: 5rem;
  }
}
#app > * {
  max-width: 52rem;
  margin-left: auto;
  margin-right: auto;
}
#app > form {
  max-width: 90%;
}
#app h1 {
  display: block;
  min-width: 90%;
  width: 90%;
  text-align: right;
  margin: 0;
  margin-bottom: 1rem;
}
</style>
```

If you check the app, you will see that our to-do list is now on a card, and our to-do items are better formatted. We can now go through and start altering our components to incorporate some of these designs.

In Vue, Add CSS Classes

The button CSS classes should be applied to the <button> in our ToDoForm component. Because Vue templates are legitimate HTML, this is accomplished in the same manner that it would be accomplished in regular HTML – by adding a class="property to the element.

Add class="btn btn__primary btn__lg" to form's <button> element:

```
<button type="submit" class="btn btn__primary btn__lg">
  Add
</button>
```

While we are here, we can do one more semantic and style update. Our form might benefit from a <h2> element because it specifies a distinct area of our website. The label, on the other hand, already indicates the form's purpose. To minimize repetition, let us enclose our label with a <h2>. There are a couple more global CSS styles that we can add. We will additionally give our <input> element the input_lg class.

Make the following changes to your ToDoForm template:

```
<template>
  <form @submit.prevent="onSubmit">
    <h2 class="label-wrapper">
      <label for="new-todo-input" class="label__lg">
        What needs to be done??
      </label>
    </h2>
    <input
      type="text"
      id="new-todo-input"
      name="new-todo"
      autocomplete="off"
      v-model.lazy.trim="label"
      class="input__lg"
    />
    <button type="submit" class="btn btn__primary
btn__lg">
      Add
    </button>
  </form>
</template>
```

Let us additionally include the stack-large class in our App.vue file's ul> tag. This will assist to increase the gap between our to-do items.

It has been updated as follows:

```
<ul aria-labelledby="list-summary"
class="stack-large">
```

Adding Scoped Styles

Our final component to style is the ToDoItem component. We may put a style> element within it to maintain the style definitions near to the component. However, if these styles change anything outside of this component, it may be difficult to trace down and correct the problem. This is where the scoped feature comes in handy; it assigns a unique HTML data attribute selector to each of your styles, preventing them from conflicting worldwide.

To utilize the scoped modifier, create a style> element at the bottom of ToDoItem.vue and give it the scoped attribute:

```
<style scoped>
</style>
```

Next, copy the following CSS into the newly created <style> element:

```
.custom-checkbox >.checkbox-label {
  font-family: Arial, sans-serif;
  -webkit-font-smoothing: antialiased;
  -moz-osx-font-smoothing: grayscale;
  font-weight: 410;
  font-size: 18px;
  font-size: 1rem;
  line-height: 1.26;
  color: #0b0c0c;
  display: block;
  margin-bottom: 6px;
}
.custom-checkbox >.checkbox {
  font-family: Arial, sans-serif;
  -webkit-font-smoothing: antialiased;
  -moz-osx-font-smoothing: grayscale;
  font-weight: 410;
  font-size: 18px;
  font-size: 1rem;
  line-height: 1.26;
  box-sizing: border-box;
  width: 90%;
  height: 42px;
  height: 2.6rem;
  margin-top: 0;
  padding: 6px;
  border: 3px solid #0b0c0c;
  border-radius: 0;
  -webkit-appearance: none;
  -moz-appearance: none;
  appearance: none;
}
```

```css
.custom-checkbox > input:focus {
  outline: 3px dashed #fd0;
  outline-offset: 0;
  box-shadow: inset 0 0 0 2px;
}
.custom-checkbox {
  font-family: Arial, sans-serif;
  -webkit-font-smoothing: antialiased;
  font-weight: 410;
  font-size: 1.8rem;
  line-height: 1.26;
  display: block;
  position: relative;
  min-height: 41px;
  margin-bottom: 12px;
  padding-left: 41px;
  clear: left;
}
.custom-checkbox > input[type="checkbox"] {
  -webkit-font-smoothing: antialiased;
  cursor: pointer;
  position: absolute;
  z-index: 1;
  top: -2px;
  left: -2px;
  width: 45px;
  height: 45px;
  margin: 0;
  opacity: 0;
}
.custom-checkbox > .checkbox-label {
  font-size: inherit;
  font-family: inherit;
  line-height: inherit;
  display: inline-block;
  margin-bottom: 0;
  padding: 9px 16px 6px;
  cursor: pointer;
  touch-action: manipulation;
}
.custom-checkbox > label::before {
  content: "";
  box-sizing: border-box;
```

```
  position: absolute;
  top: 0;
  left: 0;
  width: 41px;
  height: 41px;
  border: 3px solid currentColor;
  background: transparent;
}
.custom-checkbox > input[type="checkbox"]:focus +
label::before {
  border-width: 5px;
  outline: 4px dashed #228bec;
}
.custom-checkbox > label::after {
  box-sizing: content-box;
  content: "";
  position: absolute;
  top: 12px;
  left: 8px;
  width: 19px;
  height: 8px;
  transform: rotate(-45deg);
  border: solid;
  border-width: 0 0 6px 6px;
  border-top-color: transparent;
  opacity: 0;
  background: transparent;
}
.custom-checkbox > input[type="checkbox"]:checked +
label::after {
  opacity: 1;
}
@media only screen and (min-width: 40rem) {
  label,
  input,
  .custom-checkbox {
    font-size: 18px;
    font-size: 1.8rem;
    line-height: 1.31579;
  }
}
```

To connect the styles, we will need to add some CSS classes to our template.

Add a custom-checkbox class to the root <div>. Add a checkbox class to the <input>. Finally, add a checkbox-label class to the <label>. The modified template is provided below:

- Custom checkboxes should now be available in the app.

- CSS styling of Vue components may assist developers add design aesthetics to their applications such as background colors, text size, padding, placement, animation, and responsive displays for different screen sizes.

- Vue directives allow you to handle class and style binding within the template. To keep our application structured, you may utilize inline style within components or an external CSS file.

By creating a small web page, this lesson will look at several approaches to style Vue components with CSS.

Prerequisites

Before you begin with this instruction, there are a few things you should look for. First, you'll need a code editor, preferably Visual Studio Code. Then, in terminal, run the following command to confirm that you have Node.js version 10.x or above installed:

```
:node -v
```

You will also need Vue's most recent CLI. To download the newest version, first uninstall previous CLI version:

```
npm uninstall -g @vue/CLI
 id="or">#or
yarn global remove @vue/CLI
```

Then, install the most recent version:

```
npm install -g @vue/CLI
# OR
yarn global add @vue/CLI
```

Alternately, you can upgrade the version as follows:

```
npm update -g @vue/CLI
```

```
# OR
yarn global upgrade --latest @vue/CLI
```

Set Up Your Vue Project

To start a new project, type:

```
vue create <project_name>
```

You will then prompt to select a preset. You have three options:

1. The default setting, which includes a basic Babel + ESLint configuration.

2. Vue 3 glimpse.

3. Choose "Manually choose features" to choose the characteristics you want.

Then we will change the directory:

```
cd <project_name>
```

And we will configure ourselves to view in localhost:

```
npm run serve
```

or

```
yarn serve
```

To Style in Vue, Use the Scoped Property

The scoped property linked to the style tag below indicates that any CSS style provided here will only be applied to this template and will not be applied to any other component/template.

Create a navbar component called "Navbar" first:

```
<template>
    <div class="navbar">

        <div class="navLink">
            <a href="#">About</a>
            <a href="#">Services</a>
            <a href="#">Contact</a>
        </div>
    </div>
```

```
</template>
<script>
export default {
    name: 'Navbar'
}
</script>
<style scoped>
.navbar{
    background: #f44337;
    padding: 2rem;
    font-size: 1.7rem;
    border-bottom: 2 px solid white;


}
.navLink{
text-align: right;
}
a{
    text-decoration: none;
    padding: 1rem;
    color:#fff;
    text-align: center;
}
@media only screen and (max-width: 610px) {
    .navLink{
        display: flex;
        flex-direction: column;
    }
}
</style>
```

In the preceding example, we developed a navbar component. To style the navbar within it, we utilized a scoped property. This implies that all the CSS styles specified here will only be used in the navbar components.

Link with an External CSS File

As our application expands and additional CSS is added, I propose splitting the CSS styles into an external CSS file and tying it to the component. This is only one method for cleaning up your code.

Here is an illustration:

```
<template>
    <div class="container">
        <div class="startPage">
        <h2>Cruz Page</h2>
        <button class="btn">Get started</button>
        </div>
    </div>
</template>
<script>
export default {
    name: 'Body'
}
</script>
<style scoped src="../assets/css/startpage.css">
/* @import '../assets/css/startpage.css'; */
</style>
```

Your above component will include a link to the external CSS file listed below:

```
.startPage {
    height: 610px;
    background-color: #f44337;
    text-align: left;
}
h2{
    padding-top: 12rem;
    font-size: 5rem;
}
.btn {
    background: black;
    color: #fff;
    border-radius: 6px;
    -webkit-border-radius: 6px;
    -moz-border-radius: 6px;
    -ms-border-radius: 6px;
    -o-border-radius: 6px;
    outline: none;
    padding: 0.8rem 3rem;
    border: none;
    margin-top: 3rem;
}
```

When utilizing an external file, you can link it directly from the source file or import it in the style tag. In this example, we connected an external CSS file that we made in our Vue application's assets folder.

In Vue.js, Use Global Styles

There are assorted styles that we will wish to use across our app's components. To save time, we will utilize global styling instead of styling them in a scoped or external file (although this would work too). For general styling like as fonts, colors, background color, border-radius, and margin, global styling is your best option.

In the following example, we will add global style to our app.vue style tag.

```
<template>
  <div>
    <Navbar/>
    <Body/>
  </div>
</template>
<script>
import Navbar from './components/Navbar.vue'
import Body from './components/Body.vue'

export default {
  name: 'App',
  components: {
    Navbar,
    Body
  }
}
</script>
<style>
* {
  box-sizing: border-box;
  padding: 1;
  margin: 1;
}
h1,h2,h3,h4,h5,h6{
  color: #fff;
}
</style>
```

We used a CSS wildcard selector (pronounced as an asterisk) to pick all the items in our application, as you can see. In this case, the margin and padding on all aspects are set to 0, and the box-sizing is border-box.

Use Inline Styling

Using the style tag, inline CSS applies a unique style to a specific HTML element.

Here is an easy example:

```
<h1 style="color: yellow; text-align: center;">I am a
footer</h1>
```

We may apply an inline style to our element in Vue.js by binding the style property in the HTML tag. In this case, :style is shorthand for v-bind:style.

There are two approaches to inline styling: object syntax and array syntax. Both will be discussed in detail below.

Object Syntax

Using the object syntax, we can utilize inline styling by using the CSS attribute name as the object's key name and the values as the values of each CSS attribute. Use camelCase or "kebab-case" when using object syntax, as seen in the following example:

```
<template>
    <footer
      :style="{backgroundColor: bgColor, color:
textColor,
              height: '${height}px', textAlign: align,
              padding: '${padding}rem'
              }">
          <p> &copy; 2022</p>
    </footer>
</template>
<script>
export default {
    data(){
        return{
            bgColor: 'black',
            textColor: 'black',
            height: 220,
```

```
        align: 'center',
        padding: 6
      }
    }
}
</script>
<style>

</style>
```

We developed a footer component and then styled the footer element with object syntax.

When using the object syntax technique, it is an innovative idea to connect to a style object directly so that our template looks cleaner as our application grows. Consider the following example:

```
<template>
      <footer :style="footerStyles">
        <p> &copy; 2022</p>
      </footer>
</template>
<script>
export default {
    data(){
        return{
            footerStyles:{
                backgroundColor: 'white',
                color: 'black',
                height: '220px',
                textAlign: 'left',
                padding: '6rem'
            }

        }
    }
}
</script>
<style>

</style>
```

Array Syntax
The array syntax is used to add numerous style objects for inline styling. In the next example, we will add a new object textColor to the array syntax, which will alter the text color.

```
<template>
        <footer :style="[footerStyles1, textColor]">
        <p> &copy; 2022</p>
        </footer>
</template>
<script>
export default {
    data(){
        return{
            footerStyles1:{
                backgroundColor: 'white',
                height: '220px',
                textAlign: 'left',
                padding: '6rem'
            },
            textColor:{
                color: 'red',
            }

        }
    }
}
</script>
<style>

</style>
```

When adding numerous style objects, as demonstrated in the example above, the array syntax is ideal; to dynamically style classes, the object syntax is best for inline styling.

This section showed us how to style our Vue.js application in a variety of methods, including scoped styling, connecting to external CSS files, global styling, and inline styling with the object and array syntax.

After finishing this chapter part, we will go on to the following portion of Chapter 3, the styled components.

STYLED COMPONENTS

The style of web development frameworks has evolved in tandem with the advancement of web development capabilities and tools. Moving away from inline styles and toward CSS-in-JS solutions has improved the consistency of the development experience.

Developers can use CSS within JavaScript or JavaScript frameworks instead of producing standard separate CSS files when decorating with the styled-components library. It has had tremendous success in React, and it is now accessible for Vue applications.

Benefits of Styled Components in Vue.js

Build Your Components

Styled components allow you to create your own styled-components in Vue. To make your code more readable, you may style the HTML tags and give them a unique name.

No Classes Policy

Everything is done with the aid of props in styled components. You may modify the style of your components dynamically without requiring classes. It allows you to utilize ternary operators within the string literals of styled-components.

Concurrent Design

Styled components make it easy to keep the styling and look of your components consistent and identical across the whole application. The theming capabilities give a centralized location for identifying important design aspects such as color, size, and spacing. They can be simply incorporated into all the app's components.

A Huge Community

The styled-components community, which has seen great development, helps with any issue and has a popular library for developers.

Now that we have seen the advantages of styled components, it is time to install the library in our Vue project and learn how to use its many capabilities.

Installing Styled Components in Vue.js

Have a Vue project running on your local machine before installing the library. Install the library after creating a project using the following command:

```
npm i vue-styled-components
```

If you used the Vue CLI to create the project, the folder structure would look like this:

Structure of folder.

Helloeveryone.vue looks like this when we remove all the styles from our Vue app:

```
<template>
  <div class="hello">
    <h1>{{ msg }}</h1>
  </div>
</template>

<script>
export default {
  name: 'Helloeveryone',
  props: {
    msg: String
  }
}
</script>
```

Let us execute the project to see the results in the browser.

Welcome to Your Vue.js App

Screen of output.

As we can see, there is a basic h1 header element with no styling. We will style this h1 with styled components, thus we will need to make a new folder in the src directory to keep them. Make a Header.js file in that folder. The following is the project structure.

Then, in Header.js, add the following lines of code:

```
import styled from "vue-styled-components";

export const StyledHeader = styled.h1'
  font-size: 1.6em;
  text-align: left;
  color: red;
  background-color: lightgrey;
';
```

Finally, in Helloeveryone.vue, we can register StyledHeader and utilize it instead of h1:

```
<template>
  <div class="hello">
    <StyledHeader>{{ msg }}</StyledHeader>
  </div>
</template>

<script>
import {StyledHeader} from "../styled-components/
Header"
export default {
  name: 'Helloeveryone',
  components:{
    StyledHeader
  },
  props: {
    msg: String
  }
}
</script>
```

Now, let us start the server and see what happens to the basic and boring header tag.

As we can see, the necessary styles were implemented without the need of any CSS.

Passing the Props in Styled Components

Props may be used with styled components, just like any other component. For instance, we may build an input field and provide it a prop. In this section, we will build a new component in the components folder called Input.js and add the following code to it:

```
import styled from "vue-styled-components";

export const StyledInput = styled.input'
  font-size: 1.26em;
  padding: 0.6em;
  margin: 0.6em;
  color: violet;
  border: none;
  background-color: lavender;
  border-radius: 2px;

  &:hover {
    box-shadow: inset 2px 2px 1px rgba(0, 0, 0, 0.1);
  }
';
```

Next step is to use it in Helloeveryone.vue:

```
<template>
  <div class="hello">
    <StyledHeader>{{ msg }}</StyledHeader>
    <StyledInput/>
  </div>
</template>

<script>
import {StyledInput} from "../styled-components/Input"
import {StyledHeader} from "../styled-components/
Header"
```

```
export default {
  name: 'Helloeveryone',
  components:{
    StyledInput,StyledHeader
  },
    props: {
    msg: String
  }

}
</script>
```

Saving the changes will cause them to be reflected in the browser, indicating that our input has been rendered.

However, without sufficient input, this appears strange. Let us provide it to StyledInput as a prop along with the type.

```
<template>
  <div class="hello">
  <StyledHeader>{{ msg }}</StyledHeader>
  <StyledInput placeholder="Password" type="text"/>
  </div>
</template>
```

. . .

Dynamic Styling with Props in Vue.js

This is one of the important characteristics of stylized components. It enables developers to create dynamic styles without relying on a plethora of classes.

Because styled components may take props and apply styles depending on them, let us provide StyledHeader custom props.

Let us make the following changes to our Header.js file:

```
import styled from "vue-styled-components";
const hdrProps = { primary: Boolean };

export const StyledHeader = styled("h1", hdrProps)'
  font-size: 1.5em;
  text-align: start;
  color: ${(props) => (props.primary?  "white" :
"black")};
```

```
background-color: ${(props) => (props.primary?
"green" : "red")};
';
```

We have specified the props for our StyledHeader here. The styled function accepts as an argument the HTML element containing the props, after which we can provide the behavior of our CSS based on the value of that prop.

Let us run the project without any props to our previously built header and observe what happens in the browser.

This is operating just how we expected it to. Now, let us give our StyledHeader a main prop and see if the styles are applied correctly:

```
<template>
  <div class="hello">
  <StyledHeader primary>{{ msg }}</StyledHeader>
  <StyledInput placeholder="Password" type="text"/>
  </div>
</template>

<script>
import {StyledInput} from "../styled-components/Input"
import {StyledHeader} from "../styled-components/Header"

export default {
  name: 'Helloeveryone',
  components:{
    StyledInput,StyledHeader
  },
    props: {
    msg: String
  }

}
</script>
```

We were able to successfully adapt the style based on our assets, which provided us with the main notion behind the approach. Styles with props can be altered in response to button events, form submissions, and other events. With stylized components, we can finally harness the full potential of dynamic styling.

Applying the Same Style to Multiple Components

Styled components also allow you to make all your components look the same. This ensures that programs have a uniform style and eliminates a lot of repetitive code.

We can apply the same styles for h2 by simply adding the following line of code to Header.js:

```
export const StyledHeader2
= StyledHeader.withComponent("h2");
```

Altering the Displayed Component Dynamically

Components must sometimes vary dependent on a certain circumstance while maintaining the same styles. In this case, styled components can modify the component being rendered by using a prop.

We may change the StyledHeader to a button if we use the as prop:

```
<template>
  <div class="hello">
  <StyledHeader as=button>{{ msg }}</StyledHeader>
  <StyledInput placeholder="Password" type="text"/>
  </div>
</template>
```

Extending Styles

If we need to make changes to the component styling without changing it, we can override or add new styles.

We may override the color attribute from the previously constructed Header.js by building a new component called NewHeader.js.

Then, in NewHeader.js, add the following code:

```
import { StyledHeader } from "./Header";
export const NewHeader = StyledHeader.extend'
  color: purple;
  border-color: purple;
';
```

Let us render that and use it in our Helloeveryone.vue file now:

```
<template>
  <div class="hello">
  <StyledHeader >{{ msg }}</StyledHeader>
```

```
  <NewHeader >{{ msg }}</NewHeader>
  <StyledInput placeholder="Password" type="text"/>
  </div>
</template>

<script>
import {StyledInput} from "../styled-components/Input"
import {NewHeader} from "../styled-components/
NewHeader"

import {StyledHeader} from "../styled-components/
Header"

export default {
  name: 'Helloeveryone',
  components:{
    StyledInput,StyledHeader,NewHeader
  },
    props: {
    msg: String
  }

}
</script>
```

Styled components is a strong toolkit that solves the majority of the problems that we would encounter if we used plain CSS. While the learning curve might be severe at first, the advantages are well worth the effort.

CONCLUSION

In this chapter, we learnt about conditional, styling, and styled components, as well as what they are used for and how to use them in Vue.js. In the following chapter, we will learn about images and how to import them.

CHAPTER 4

Working with Images

IN THIS CHAPTER

➤ Images

➤ Importing images

In Chapter 3, we discussed conditional, styling, and styled-components in Vue.js, as well as what they are used for and how to utilize them.

In this chapter, we will learn about images and importing images. Let us go directly and know how to import pictures and use them in Vue.js.

IMPORTING IMAGES

As simple as:

```
<template>
    <div id="app">
        <img src="./assets/logo.png">
    </div>
</template>

<script>
    export default {
    }
</script>

<style lang="css">
</style>
```

DOI: 10.1201/9781003310464-4

They are taken from the project generated by vue cli.

If you intend to utilize your picture as a module, remember to connect data to your Vue.js component:

```
<template>
    <div id="app">
        <img :src="image"/>
    </div>
</template>

<script>
    import image from "./assets/logo.png"

    export default {
        data: function () {
            return {
                image: image
            }
        }
    }
</script>

<style lang="css">
</style>
```

And a shorter version:

```
<template>
    <div id="app">
        <img :src="require('./assets/logo.png')"/>
    </div>
</template>

<script>
    export default {
    }
</script>

<style lang="css">
</style>
```

It is heavily suggested to use webpack when importing pictures from assets and in general for optimization and pathing purposes.

If you want to load them by webpack, you can use: src='require('path/to/file') otherwise, it will not execute the required statement as Javascript.

In typescript you can do the exact same operation: :src="require('@/assets/image.png')".

Why is the following considered bad practice?

```
<template>
  <div id="app">
    <img src="./assets/logo.png">
  </div>
</template>

<script>
export default {
}
</script>

<style lang="scss">
</style>
```

When building with the Vue CLI, webpack cannot guarantee that the assets file will retain the relative importing structure. This is due to webpack attempting to optimize and chunk objects found within the assets folder. If you want to utilize a relative import, navigate to the static folder and use: img src="./static/logo.png">.

I recently encountered this problem when working with Typescript. If you are using Typescript like I do, you will need to import the following assets:

```
<img src="@/assets/images/logo.png" alt="">
```

Here are some questions people ask when working on Vue.js with answers.

How can you include photos in my .vue single file components?

```
<template>
  <img v-bind:src="require('images/rails.png')" />
</template>
```

How can I add images to the data object Vue.js?

```
<template>
  <div id="app">
    <img :src="image" />
  </div>
</template>
<script>
import image from "./assets/logo.png"

export default {
  data: function () {
    return {
      image: image
    }
  }
}
</script>
```

How to upload images to Vue.js?

First, choose a file (remember to include <input type="file"> in your component template code).

Then, in your .vue component, you will need the "two handler methods":

```
methods: {
  onFileChanged (event) {
  const file = event.target.files[0]
},

onUpload() {
// upload the file
}
```

The file is then sent to a server (you can use Axios).

You can submit the file in state as binary data or wrapped in a form data object.

As binary data:

```
onUpload() {
  axios.post('my-domain.com/file-upload', this.
selectedFile)
}
```

As form data:

```
onUpload() {
  const formData = new FormData()
  formData.append('myFile', this.selectedFile, this.
selectedFile.name)
  axios.post('my-domain.com/file-upload', formData)
}
```

That's all there is to it! Image has been posted!

How do you insert a background image in Vue?

You can use inline styles to add a background picture in a variety of methods, but here's an example of doing so by placing the style object within a Vue data property:

```
<template>
  <div :style="image"></div>
</template>

<script>
export default {
  data() {
    return {
      image: { backgroundImage: "url(https://vuejs
.org/images/logo.png)" }
    };
  }
};
</script>
```

Here's an example if your backdrop image is generated by your backend server:

```
<template>
  <div :style="{backgroundImage:'url(${post.
image})'}"></div>
</template>
```

How can you send variables to inline background images in .vue?

It is simple to pass a style binding into Vue! You can do it like this:

```
<div v-bind:style="{ color: activeColor, fontSize:
fontSize + 'px' }"></div>
```

Alternatively, you can utilize the variable directly as follows:

```
<template>
  <div class="progress">
    <div class="progress__fill" :style="{ width:
progress }"></div>
  </div>
</template>

<script>
  export default {
    props: ["percent"],
    data() {
      return {
        progress: this.percent + "%",
      };
    },
  };
</script>
```

But, if the background picture is reliant on the data binding, how would you transfer the data?

If you have static data, you can import it into Vue data binding and feed to it.

```
<template>
  <div
    class=" bg-no-repeat bg-cover  bg-white hero
relative"
    :style="{ backgroundImage: 'url(${backgroundUrl})'
}"
  ></div>
</template>
<script>
import backgroundUrl from "~/assets/img/bg-wp.png";
export default {
  data() {
    return {
      backgroundUrl,
    };
  },
};
</script>
```

If you have dynamic data, you may send the variable straight into the inline-style.

```
<template>
  <div
    class="min-h-screen bg-grey bg-cover flex items-
end block md:fixed w-full md:w-1/2 shadow-md"
    :style="{ backgroundImage: 'url(${member.
coverImage})' }" >
    <p>{{ member.name }}</p>
  </div>
</template>
<script>
export default {
  data() {
    return {
      member: {
          name: "Jakz",
          coverImage: "<https://vuejs.org/images/logo
.png>",
      },
    };
  },
};
</script>
```

CONCLUSION

In this chapter, we learned about how we can import images and use them in Vue.js. The following chapter will go over routing and routing parameters.

CHAPTER 5

Routing in Vue

IN THIS CHAPTER

➤ Routing

➤ Routing and query parameters

We discussed how to import pictures and use them in Vue.js in the Chapter 4. We will learn about routing and routing parameters in this chapter.

ROUTING

Vue.js has a slew of tools for creating reusable web components. One of these ways is routing. It enables the user to navigate between pages without refreshing the page. This is what makes your web apps' navigation appealing and straightforward.

Getting Started

So, let us get our Vue.js Router project started by installing and starting a new Vue.js project. We will need Node.js installed. To create a new Vue.js project, we will use vue-cli. Take the following steps.

Run the following code in your terminal:

```
vue init webpack vue-router

//
cd vue-router
//
npm run dev
```

DOI: 10.1201/9781003310464-5

Browse to http://localhost:8080

Welcome to Your Vue.js App

Essential Links

Core Docs   Forum   Community Chat   Twitter
Docs for This Template

Ecosystem

vue-router   vuex   vue-loader   awesome-vue

Screen of welcome.

In your text editor, open the app. Open the Helloeveryone.vue file in the components folder and proceed as follows:

- Home.vue should be renamed Helloeveryone.vue. Delete all code and replace it with the following:

```
<template>
  <div class="home">
    <h1>Home</h1>
  </div>
</template>

<script>
export default {
  name: 'home',
  data () {
    return {
      msg: 'Welcome to Vue.js App'
    }
  }
}
</script>

<!-- Add the "scoped" property to restrict CSS to
only this component. -->
<style scoped>

</style>
```

- Replace Helloeveryone with home in index.js within the router folder:

```
import Vue from 'vue'
import Router from 'vue-router'
import home from '@/components/home'

Vue.use(Router)

export default new Router({
  routes: [
    {
      path: '/',
      name: 'home',
      component: home
    }
  ]
})
```

The App.vue file should look something like this:

```
<template>
  <div id="app">

    <router-view/>
  </div>
</template>

<script>
export default {
  name: 'App'
}
</script>

<style>
#app {

}
</style>
```

Now it's time to write some code!

We are planning to implement a Bootswatch template now. You are allowed to use whatever template you choose. I will go with Cosmo.

To inspect the code source, use Ctrl + U and just copy the Navbar (we just need the navbar). Copy and paste this code into the App.vue component.

Next, we will add three more components: a blog, services, and a contact.

Make a new file called blog.vue in the components folder and paste the following code into it:

```
<template>
 <div class="blog">
  <h1>{{blog}}</h1>
 </div>
</template>
<script>
 export default{
  name:'blog',
  data (){
   return{
    title:'Blog'
   }
  }
 }
</script>
<style scoped>
</style>
```

If you want to do same thing with the service and contact components, make sure your component folder has the following files:

- home.vue

- blog.vue

- services.vue

- contact.vue

Router's Config

After we have created these four components, we must configure the routers so that we may browse between them.

So, how do we use the routers to go to each component?

We must first grasp the routing rules. Now open index.js to make some modifications within the router folder.

Take the following steps:

- Begin by importing your components into index.js. Using the import method, import all the components.

```
import home from '@/components/home'
import blog from '@/components/blog'
import services from '@/components/services'
import contact from '@/components/contact'
```

- Second, import Vue and the router module from vue-router:

```
import Vue from 'vue'
import Router from 'vue-router'

// use router
Vue.use(Router)
```

If you installed Vue via vue-cli, the vue-router module will be imported by default.

- Finally, inside the router folder, we must configure the routers for them to function. The router method accepts an Array of objects, which in turn takes the attributes of each component:

```
export default new Router({
  routes: [
    {
      path: '/',
      name: 'home',
      component: home
    },
    {
      path: '/blog',
      name: 'blog',
      component: blog
    },
    {
      path: '/services',
      name: 'services',
      component: services
    },
    {
```

```
      path: '/contact',
      name: 'contact',
      component: contact
    }
  ]
})
```

- **path:** path of the component

- **name:** name of the component

- **component:** view of the component

To make any component the default component, set the path attribute to slash('/'):

```
path:'/'
```

In our example, we made the home page the default. When you start the project in the browser, the home page will be the first page that appears.

```
{
  path:'/',
  name:'home',
  component:home
}
```

The vue-router contains more complex parameters and methods, but we are not going to get into that right now.

The following are the attributes and methods that may be used with vue-router:

- Nested routers

- Named view

- Redirect and Alias

- Navigation guard

- Router instance

You may now browse to any component by entering the component's name.

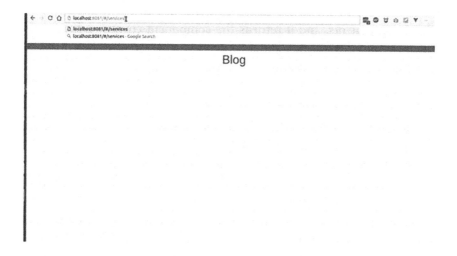

Example of blog page.

Router-Link

Now we will configure the navigation using the Navbar we constructed with the router-link element.

To accomplish so, we should replace the </a> element with <router-link>/router/link>, as seen below:

```
<li class="nav-item">
  <router-link class="nav-link" to="/blog">Blog</
router-link>
</li>
<li class="nav-item">
  <router-link class="nav-link" to="/
services">Services</router-link>
 </li>
<li class="nav-item">
   <router-link class="nav-link" to="/
contact">contact</router-link>
 </li>
```

The router-link accepts the to='path' property, which accepts the component's path as a value.

Router-View

The <router-view> tag may find in the App.vue file. It is the perspective in which the components are rendered. It is like the main div, which includes all the components, and it returns the component corresponding to the current route. We will talk about route-view when we use the animation transition in the future section.

Using the Parameters Inside the Routers

At this stage, we will go to individual components using parameters. The parameters allow the routing to be dynamic.

We will make a list of products and an array of data to deal with parameters. When you click on a product link, it will lead us to the page information through a parameter.

In this case, we will not utilize a database or an API to get product data. So we need to establish an Array of items that will serve as a database.

Within the home, put the Array in the data() function of the Vue component as follows:

```
export default {
  name: 'home',
  data () {
    return {
      title: 'Home',
      products:[
      {
        productTitle:"ABC",
        image        : require('../assets/images/
product1.png'),
        productId:1
      },
      {
        productTitle:"KARA",
        image        : require('../assets/images/
product2.png'),
        productId:2
      },
      {
        productTitle:"Tin",
        image        : require('../assets/images/
product3.png'),
```

```
        productId:3
      },
      {
        productTitle:"EFGH",
        image        : require('../assets/images/
product4.png'),
        productId:4
      },
      {
        productTitle:"MLIT",
        image        : require('../assets/images/
product5.png'),
        productId:5
      },
      {
        productTitle:"Banana",
        image        : require('../assets/images/
product6.png'),
        productId:6
      }
     ]
   }
  }
}
```

Then, using the v-for directive, fetch and loop through the Products Array.

```
<div class="row">
    <div class="col-md-4 col-lg4"
v-for="(data,index) in products" :key="index">
      <img :src="data.image" class="img-fluid">
       <h3>{{data.productTitle}}</h3>
    </div>
   </div>
```

To get to the details component, we must first add a click event:

```
<h3 @click="goTodetail()" >{{data.productTitle}}
</h3>
```

Then include the following methods:

```
methods:{
  goTodetail() {
    this.$router.push({name:'details'})
  }
```

If you click the title, it will return undefined since the details component has not yet been built. So, let us make one:

```
details.vue
```

```
<template>
 <div class="details">
  <div class="container">
   <h1 class="text-primary text-center">{{title}}</h1>
  </div>
 </div>
</template>
<script>
 export default{
  name:'details',
  data(){
   return{
    title:"details"
    }
   }
  }
</script>
```

How can we navigate to the details page and retrieve the matching data if we do not have a database?

The same products array will use in the details component. As a result, we can extract the id from the URL:

```
products:[
      {
        productTitle:"ABC",
        image        : require('../assets/images/
product1.png'),
        productId:1
      },
      {
```

```
      productTitle: "KARA",
      image        : require ('../assets/images/
product2.png'),
      productId: 2
    },
    {
      productTitle: "Tin",
      image        : require ('../assets/images/
product3.png'),
      productId: 3
    },
    {
      productTitle: "EFGH",
      image        : require ('../assets/images/
product4.png'),
      productId: 4
    },
    {
      productTitle: "MLIT",
      image        : require ('../assets/images/
product5.png'),
      productId: 5
    },
    {
      productTitle: "Banana",
      image        : require ('../assets/images/
product6.png'),
      productId: 6
    }
    ]
```

First, we must pass the id as a parameter to the goTodetail() method:

```
<h3 @click="goTodetail (data.productId) " >{{data.
productTitle}}</h3>
```

Then, to the router method, add a second argument.

The $router function accepts two parameters: the name of the component to which we want to go and the id parameter (or any other parameter).

```
this.$router.push({name: 'details',params:{Pid:proId}})
```

Insert Pid as a parameter into index.js in the router folder:

```
{
  path: '/details/:Pid',
  name: 'details',
  component: details
  }
```

home.vue

```
methods:{
  goTodetail(prodId) {
    this.$router.push({name:'details',params:{Pid:
proId}})
  }
  }
```

Use the following code to obtain the matching parameter:

```
this.$route.params.Pid
```

details.vue

```
<h2>the product id is :{{this.$route.params.Pid}}</h2>
```

Then, in detalils.vue, loop over the products array and find the item that matches the parameter Pid and provide its data:

```
<div class="col-md-12" v-for="(product,index) in
products" :key="index">
    <div v-if="proId == product.productId">
    <h1>{{product.productTitle}}</h1>
    <img :src="product.image" class="img-fluid">
    </div>
    </div>

///
export default{
  name:'details',
  data(){
   return{
    proId:this.$route.params.Pid,
```

```
     title:"details"
       }
   }
}
```

detail.vue Component

```
<template>
 <div class="details">
  <div class="container">
   <div class="row">
    <div class="col-md-12" v-for="(product,index) in
products" :key="index">
     <div v-if="proId == product.productId">
      <h1>{{product.productTitle}}</h1>
      <img :src="product.image" class="img-fluid">
     </div>
    </div>
   </div>
  </div>
 </div>
</template>
<script>
 export default{
  name:'details',
  data(){
   return{
    proId:this.$route.params.Pid,
    title:"details",
    products:[
    {
    productTitle:"ABC",
    image       : require('../assets/images/product1.
png'),
    productId:1
    },
    {
    productTitle:"KARA",
    image       : require('../assets/images/product2.
png'),
    productId:2
    },
    {
```

```
    productTitle:"Tin",
    image      : require('../assets/images/product3.
png'),
    productId:3
    },
    {
    productTitle:"EFGH",
    image      : require('../assets/images/product4.
png'),
    productId:4
    },
    {
    productTitle:"MLIT",
    image      : require('../assets/images/product5.
png'),
    productId:5
    },
    {
    productTitle:"Banana",
    image      : require('../assets/images/product6.
png'),
    productId:6
    }
    ]


    }
   }
  }
</script>
```

The Transition

In this section, we will add an animation transition to the animated component. We will animate the component transition. It improves the navigation and gives a better UX and UI.

To create an animation transition, place the "router-view>" element within the "<transition/>" tag and give it a class name.

App.vue

```
<transition name="moveInUp">
        <router-view/>
  </transition>
```

Add enter-active to the transition tag's name to animate the component's transition when it enters the view. Then add leave-active and give it the CSS transition settings as shown below:

```
.moveInUp-enter-active{
  opacity: 0;
  transition: opacity 1s ease-in;
}
```

Using CSS3 Animation

Now we will animate with @keyframes in CSS3.

Add a fading effect to the view when the component enters it.

```
.moveInUp-enter-active{
  animation: fadeIn 1s ease-in;
}
@keyframes fadeIn{
  0%{
    opacity: 0;
  }
  60%{
    opacity: 0.5;
  }
  90%{
    opacity: 1;
  }
}
```

When the component exits the view, add another fading effect.

When the component exits the view, we will make it go in and up.

```
.moveInUp-leave-active{
  animation: moveInUp .3s ease-in;
}
@keyframes moveInUp{
 0%{
  transform: translateY(0);
 }
  100%{
  transform: translateY(-410px);
 }
}
```

You may now customize the animations and transitions for your components.

Vue.js lacks a built-in router feature. To install it, we will need to do a few additional steps.

Direct Download from CDN

The most recent version of vue-router may find at https://unpkg.com/vue-router/dist/vue-router.js.

Unpkg.com gives cdn links based on npm. The URL above is always up to date with the most recent version. As seen below, we can download and host it and then utilize it with a script tag and vue.js.

```
<script src = "/path/to/vue.js"></script>
<script src = "/path/to/vue-router.js"></script>
```

- **Using the NPM:** To install the vue-router, use the following command:

  ```
  npm install vue-router
  ```

- **Using the GitHub:** We may clone the repository from GitHub by doing the following:

  ```
  git clone https://github.com/vuejs/vue-router.git
  node_modules/vue-router
  ```

  ```
  cd node_modules/vue-router
  ```

  ```
  npm install
  ```

  ```
  npm run build
  ```

Let's start with a basic example that makes use of vue-router.js.

```
<html>
   <head>
      <title>VueJs Instance</title>
      <script type = "text/javascript" src = "js/vue.js"></script>
      <script type = "text/javascript" src = "js/vue-router.js"></script>
   </head>
   <body>
```

```
<div id = "app">
    <h1>RoutingExample</h1>
    <p>
        <router-link to = "/route1">Router Link
1</router-link>
        <router-link to = "/route2">Router Link
2</router-link>
    </p>
    <!-- route outlet -->
    <!-- The route-matched component will be
rendered here. -->
    <router-view></router-view>
</div>
<script type = "text/javascript">
    const Route1 = { template: '<div style =
"border-radius:21px;background-color:cyan;width:210px;
height:50px;margin:12px;font-
size:26px;padding:12px;">This is router 1</div>' }
    const Route2 = { template: '<div style =
"border-radius:21px;background-color:green;width:210px
;height:50px;margin:12px;font-
size:26px;padding:12px;">This is router 2</div>' }
    const routes = [
        { path: '/route1', component: Route1 },
        { path: '/route2', component: Route2 }
    ];
    const router = new VueRouter({
        routes // short for 'routes: routes'
    });
    var vm = new Vue({
        el: '#app',
        router
    });
</script>
</body>
</html>
```

To begin with routing, we must include the vue-router.js file. Save the code from https://unpkg.com/vue-router/dist/vue-router.js to the file vue-router.js. The script comes after vue. Js in the following way:

```
<script type = "text/javascript" src = "js/vue.js"></
script>
<script type = "text/javascript" src = "js/vue-router.
js"></script>
```

A router link is defined in the body section as follows:

```
<p>
    <router-link   to = "/route1">Router Link 1</
router-link>
    <router-link   to = "/route2">Router Link 2</
router-link>
</p>
```

The component <router-link> is used to browse to the HTML content that will be shown to the user. The "to property" specifies the destination, i.e., the source file from which the displayed contents will be selected.

We built two router connections in the preceding code.

Examine the script area where the router is configured. The following two constants are created:

```
const   Route1 = { template: '<div style = "border-
radius:21px;background-color:cyan;width:210px;height:6
0px;margin:12px;font-size:26px;padding:12px;">This is
router 1</div>' };
const Route2 = { template: '<div style = "border-
radius:21px;background-color:green;width:210px;height:
60px;margin:12px;font-size:26px;padding:12px;">This is
router 2</div>' }
```

They have templates that must be displayed when the router link is clicked.

Following that is the routes const, which determines the path that will present in the URL.

```
const routes = [
    { path: '/route1', component: Route1 },
    { path: '/route2', component: Route2 }
];
```

Routes specify both the route and the component. When the user clicks on the router link, the path, /route1, will be shown in the URL ("VueJS - Routing - Tutorialspoint").

The names of the templates are sent to the component to be shown. The path from the routes must match the path from the router to the property.

For instance, <router-link **to = "path here"**></router-link>

The instance of VueRouter is then created using the following code.

```
const router = new VueRouter({
    routes // short for the 'routes: routes'
});
```

The routes are passed as parameters to the VueRouter constructor. The router object is allocated to the main Vue instance using the code below.

```
var vm = new Vue({
    el: '#app',
    router
});
```

Run the example to view the result in the browser. When we inspect and test the router link, we discover that it adds class to the active element.

class = "router-link-exact-active router-link-active" has been added. As demonstrated in the above example, the active link receives the class. Another thing to keep in mind is that the <router-link> is produced as a tag.

Props for Router Link

Let us have a look at some other characteristics that may be given to <router-link>.

This is the path to the destination <router-link>. When clicked, the value of to is sent internally to router.push(). The value must be either a string or a location object. When we use an object, we must bind it, as demonstrated in second example.

First example:

```
<router-link to = "/route1">Router Link 1</
router-link>
renders as
<a href = "#/route">Router Link </a>
```

Second example:

```
<router-link v-bind:to = "{path:'/route1'}">Router
Link 1</router-link>
```

Third example:

```
<router-link v-bind:to =
  "{path:'/route1', query: { name: 'Tery'
}}">Router Link 1</router-link>//router link with
query string.
```

The query string name = Tery appears in the URL route. For example, http://localhost/vueexamples/vue router.html#/route1?name = Tery

When you add replace to a router link, it will call router.replace() instead of router.push(). The navigation history is not saved when using replace.

Example:

```
"<router-link v-bind:to = "{path:'/route1', query:
{ name: 'Tery' }}"   replace>Router Link 1</
router-link>" ("VueJS - Routing - Tutorialspoint")
```

append

By appending to the router-link>router-link>, the path is made relative.

If we want to go from the router link with path /route1 to the router link with path /route2, the path in the browser will be /route1/route2.

Example:

```
<router-link v-bind:to = "{ path: '/route1'}"
append>Router Link 1</router-link> tag
```

<router-link> is currently rendered as a tag. If we wish to render it as another tag, we must specify it using tag = "tagname";

```
<p>
   <router-link v-bind:to = "{ path: '/route1'}" tag =
"span">Router Link 1</router-link>
   <router-link v-bind:to = "{ path: '/route2'}" tag =
"span">Router Link 2</router-link>
</p>
```

The tag span has been set, and this is what is displayed in the browser.

The tag that is now shown is a span tag. We will still notice the click when we go by clicking on the router link.

active-class

When the router link is active, the active class that is added is router-link-active by default. We may override the class by setting it as seen in the following code.

```
<style>
    ._active{
        background-color : black;
    }
</style>
<p>
    <router-link v-bind:to = "{ path: '/route1'}"
active-class = "_active">Router Link 1</router-link>
    <router-link v-bind:to = "{ path: '/route2'}" tag =
"span">Router Link 2</router-link>
</p>
```

The class used is active_class ="_active". This is output displayed in the browser.

exact-active-class

The router-link-exact-active class is used by default. We may replace it with exact-active-class.

```
<p>
    <router-link v-bind:to = "{ path: '/route1'}"
exact-active-class = "_active">Router Link 1</
router-link>
    <router-link v-bind:to = "{ path: '/route2'}" tag =
"span">Router Link 2</router-link>
</p>
```

The default event for router-link is currently the click event. Using the event property, we can adjust this.

Example:

```
<router-link v-bind:to = "{ path: '/route1'}"
event = "mouseover">Router Link 1</router-link>
```

Simple Routing from Scratch

If you simply require basic routing and do not want to use a full-featured router package, you may accomplish it by dynamically displaying a page-level component like this:

```
const NotFound = { template: '<p>Page not found</p>' }
const Home = { template: '<p>home page</p>' }
const About = { template: '<p>about page</p>' }

const routes = {
  '/': Home,
  '/about': About
}

new Vue({
  el: '#app',
  data: {
    currentRoute: window.location.pathname
  },
  computed: {
    ViewComponent () {
      return routes[this.currentRoute] || NotFound
    }
  },
  render (h) { return h(this.ViewComponent) }
})
```

When used with the HTML5 History API, you may create a simple but completely working client-side router.

ROUTER AND QUERY PARAMETERS

When utilizing routes with params, keep in mind that the same component instance will be reused when user navigates from /user/foo to /user/bar. Because both methods produce the same component, this is more efficient than deleting the previous instance and then recreating it. However, this also implies that the component's lifecycle hooks will not be invoked.

To respond to changes in parameters in the same component, just watch the $route object:

```
const User = {
  template: '...',
```

```
  watch: {
    $route(to, from) {
      // react to route changes
    }
  }
}
```

Alternatively, utilize the beforeRouteUpdate navigation guard, which was added in 2.2:

```
const User = {
  template: '...',
  beforeRouteUpdate(to, from, next) {
    // react to route changes...
    // do not forget to call next()
  }
}
```

Getting query parameters from a URL are something we must do rather frequently in our Vue.js projects.

We will look at how to obtain query parameters from a URL in Vue.js in the following section.

Get Query Parameters from a URL

We can simply obtain a query parameter in a route component's URL using Vue Router.

For example, we could write:

main.js

```
import Vue from "vue";
import App from "./App.vue";
import Helloeveryone from "./views/Helloeveryone.vue";
import VueRouter from "vue-router";

const routes = [{ path: "/hello", component:
Helloeveryone }];

Vue.config.productionTip = false;
Vue.use(VueRouter);
```

```
const router = new VueRouter({
  routes
});

new Vue({
  render: (h) => h(App),
  router
}).$mount("#app");
```

App.vue

```
<template>
  <div id="app">
    <router-view></router-view>
  </div>
</template>

<script>
export default {
  name: "App",
};
</script>
```

views/Helloeveryone.vue

```
<template>
  <div class="hello">
    <h1>hi, {{ name }}</h1>
  </div>
</template>

<script>
export default {
  name: "Helloeveryone",
  data() {
    return {
      name: "",
    };
  },
  mounted() {
    this.name = this.$route.query.name;
  },
};
</script>
```

In main.js, we defined the routes array, which contains the routes that may be loaded using Vue Router.

Then we call Vue.use(VueRouter) to add dependencies such as router-view and additional attributes for components.

Following that, we construct a VueRouter object with the routes.

To register the routes, we feed the router into the Vue instance object.

We acquire the query parameter name the same way we did in views/Helloeveryone.vue.

this.$router.query.name contains the value of the query parameter name.

As a result, when we navigate to /#/hello?

We see "hello, jamy" displayed since we assigned it to this.name.

Another option is to send the query text as props.

To do this, we write:

main.js

```
import Vue from "vue";
import App from "./App.vue";
import Helloeveryone from "./views/Helloeveryone.
vue";
import VueRouter from "vue-router";

const routes = [
  {
    path: "/hello",
    component: Helloeveryone,
    props: (route) => ({ name: route.query.name })
  }
];
Vue.config.productionTip = false;
Vue.use(VueRouter);
const router = new VueRouter({
  routes
});
new Vue({
  render: (h) => h(App),
  router
}).$mount("#app");
```

Then we change views/Helloeveryone.vue to:

```
<template>
  <div class="hello">
    <h1>hi, {{ name }}</h1>
  </div>
</template>

<script>
export default {
  name: "Helloeveryone",
  props: {
    name: String,
  },
};
</script>
```

And App.vue remains unchanged.

The props property has been set to a function that accepts the route parameter.

And we return an object with the route.query.name attribute set.

We register the name prop with the props property in Helloeveryone. vue and show the name directly in the template.

As a result, when we go to /#/hello?name=jamy, we see "hey, jamy" once more.

URLSearchParams

If we do not want to utilize Vue Router, we may use the URLSearchParams constructor to access the query parameter.

For example, we could write:

main.js

```
import Vue from "vue";
import App from "./App.vue";
Vue.config.productionTip = false;
new Vue({
  render: (h) => h(App)
}).$mount("#app");
```

App.vue

```
<template>
  <div id="app">
    <Helloeveryone />
  </div>
</template>

<script>
import Helloeveryone from "./components/
Helloeveryone";

export default {
  name: "App",
  components: {
    Helloeveryone,
  },
};
</script>
```

components/Helloeveryone.vue

```
<template>
  <div class="hello">
    <h1>hi, {{ name }}</h1>
  </div>
</template>

<script>
export default {
  name: "Helloeveryone",
  data() {
    return {
      name: "",
    };
  },
  mounted() {
    const urlParams = new URLSearchParams(window.
location.search);
    this.name = urlParams.get("name");
  },
};
</script>
```

The query string is sent to the URLSearchParams constructor through window.location.search.

Then, using urlParams.get, we can retrieve the query parameter with the specified key.

We gave it the name this.name so that we could use it in the template.

So, if we go to /?name=jamy, we see "hi, jamy."

CONCLUSION

In this chapter, we learnt about routing in Vue.js, as well as what routers and parameters are and how they are utilized. The following chapter will teach us about programmatic navigation.

CHAPTER 6

Programmatic Navigation

IN THIS CHAPTER

➤ Programmatic navigation

➤ Lazy loading

In Chapter 5, we studied about routing in Vue.js, as well as what router and parameter are and how they are utilized. This chapter will teach us about programmatic navigation and lazy loading.

PROGRAMMATIC NAVIGATION

Vue.js is a basic web app framework for developing interactive front-end projects.

This piece will look at how to traverse through Vue Router routes dynamically.

Programmatic Routes

We can explore routes programmatically and use a router-link to generate a link that allows users to navigate routes.

router.push(location, onComplete?, onAbort?)

To do this, we may use a component's $router object to navigate routes programmatically.

DOI: 10.1201/9781003310464-6

When a router-link is clicked, Router. Push (...) is called. We can use it to go to routes programmatically.

For example, we can programmatically construct and travel across routes as follows:

```
src/index.js :
const Foo = { template: "<p>foo</p>" };
const Bar = { template: "<p>bar</p>" };const routes =
[
  {
    path: "/foo",
    component: Foo
  },
  {
    path: "/bar",
    component: Bar
  }
];const router = new VueRouter({
  routes
});new Vue({
  el: "#app",
  router,
  methods: {
    goTo(route) {
      this.$router.push(route);
    }
  }
});
```

```
index.html :
<!DOCTYPE html>
<html>
  <head>
    <title>App</title>
    <meta charset="UTF-8" />
    <script src="https://unpkg.com/vue/dist/vue.js"></
script>
    <script src="https://unpkg.com/vue-router/dist/
vue-router.js"></script>
  </head>
  <body>
    <div id="app">
      <div>
```

```
        <a href="#" @click='goTo("foo")'>Foo</a>
        <a href="#" @click='goTo("bar")'>Bar</a>
      </div>
      <router-view></router-view>
    </div>
    <script src="src/index.js"></script>
  </body>
</html>
```

The goTo function in the above code accepts a string representing the path we wish to go.

In the method, we use this.$router.push(route); in the method.

So we see Foo when we click on it, and Bar when we click on it.

We may also send an object in the following way:

```
this.$router.push({ path: route });
```

Also, when $ router.Push, we can travel to designated routes. To do this, we write:

```
src/index.js :
const Foo = { template: "<p>foo</p>" };
const Bar = { template: "<p>bar</p>" };const routes = [
  {
    name: "foo",
    path: "/foo",
    component: Foo
  },
  {
    name: "bar",
    path: "/bar",
    component: Bar
  }
];const router = new VueRouter({
  routes
});new Vue({
  el: "#app",
  router,
  methods: {
    goTo(name) {
      this.$router.push({ name });
    }
  }
});
```

```
index.html :
<!DOCTYPE html>
<html>
  <head>
    <title>App</title>
    <meta charset="UTF-8" />
    <script src="https://unpkg.com/vue/dist/vue.js"></
script>
    <script src="https://unpkg.com/vue-router/dist/
vue-router.js"></script>
  </head>
  <body>
    <div id="app">
      <div>
        <a href="#" @click='goTo("foo")'>Foo</a>
        <a href="#" @click='goTo("bar")'>Bar</a>
      </div>
      <router-view></router-view>
    </div>
    <script src="src/index.js"></script>
  </body>
</html>
```

We defined named routes in the preceding code by adding the name attribute to our routes and writing:

```
const routes = [
{
name: "foo",
path: "/foo",
component: Foo
},
{
name: "bar",
path: "/bar",
component: Bar
}
];
```

Then, in the goTo method, we may go to a route by name as follows:

```
this.$router.push({ name });
```

We can include the following route parameters:

```
router.push({ name: 'user', params: { userId: '123' } })
```

The following methods will not work:

```
router.push({ path: 'user', params: { userId: '123' } })
```

We may use the following query strings to go to routes:

```
router.push({ path: 'user', query: { userId: '123' } })
```

or:

```
router.push({ name: 'user', query: { userId: '123' } })
```

We can also go on a path with a route parameter as follows:

```
router.push({ path: '/user/123' });
```

We can utilize them in the following ways, for example:

```
const Foo = { template: "<p>foo {{$route.query.id}}</
p>" };
const Bar = { template: "<p>bar</p>" };const routes =
[
  {
    path: "/foo",
    component: Foo
  },
  {
    path: "/bar",
    component: Bar
  }
];const router = new VueRouter({
  routes
});new Vue({
  el: "#app",
  router,
  methods: {
    goTo(path, query) {
      this.$router.push({ path, query });
```

```
    }
  }
});
```

When we click on Foo, we see foo 1 since we use a query string with id as the key.

It is the same as entering /#/foo?id=1 into your browser.

The same rules apply to the router-link component's property.

We can supply an onComplete and onAbort callback to the router with Vue Router 2.2.0 or later. Either push or router. Replace with the second and third parameters.

In Vue Router 3.1.0 or later. Router and push. Because replace returns promises, we do not need to pass in the second and third parameters to address such scenarios.

If our destination is the same as the current route but only the parameters change, such as /users/1 to /users/2, we must utilize the beforeRoute-Update hook to respond to changes.

router.replace(location, onComplete?, onAbort?)

router.replace acts like router.push except that no new history entry is added.

router.replace(…) is same as <router-link :to="…" replace> .

router.go(n)

We may make use of the router.go ahead or backward by specifying the number of steps to take forward or backward. Positive is ahead, and negative is backward.

We may utilize it in the following ways, for example:

```
src/index.js :
const Foo = { template: "<p>foo</p>" };
const Bar = { template: "<p>bar</p>" };const routes = [
  {
    path: "/foo",
    component: Foo
  },
  {
    path: "/bar",
    component: Bar
  }
```

```
];const router = new VueRouter({
  routes
});new Vue({
  el: "#app",
  router,
  methods: {
    forward() {
      this.$router.go(-1);
    },
    back() {
      this.$router.go(1);
    }
  }
});
```

```
index.html :
<!DOCTYPE html>
<html>
  <head>
    <title>App</title>
    <meta charset="UTF-8" />
    <script src="https://unpkg.com/vue/dist/vue.js"></
script>
    <script src="https://unpkg.com/vue-router/dist/
vue-router.js"></script>
  </head>
  <body>
    <div id="app">
      <div>
        <router-link to="foo">Foo</router-link>
        <router-link to="bar">Bar</router-link>
        <a href="#" @click="forward">Forward</a>
        <a href="#" @click="back">Back</a>
      </div>
      <router-view></router-view>
    </div>
    <script src="src/index.js"></script>
  </body>
</html>
```

To go ahead and backward, we must use the forward and reverse procedures, respectively.

If no such history record exists, router.go will fail quietly.

To navigate to a path with alternative names, pathways, query strings, or arguments, we use the router.push function.

We can do the same thing with the router. Replace but do not create a new history item.

They both accept a string or object for the route, as well as handlers for onComplete and onAbort.

Router.go allows us to go through the browser's history. To go ahead or backward, a series of steps must be taken.

router.push()

You may utilize the router instance's router.push() function. Consider the following examples:

```
// literal string path
router.push('home')

// object
router.push({ path: 'home' })

// named route
router.push({ name: 'user', params: { userId: '123' } })

// with query, resulting in /register?plan=private
router.push({ path: 'register', query: { plan:
'private' } })
```

router.push() example

Assume the user has just finished filling out a form. If no faults are found, the user should be sent to the homepage. We can do this by first validating the form and then navigating the user to the homepage using the router. push() function. Consider the following example:

```
methods: {
submit() {
if (this.$refs.form.validate()) {
router.push({ path: 'home' })
}
}
}
```

Aside from utilizing <router-link> to build anchor tags for declarative navigation, we can also use the router's instance functions programmatically.

```
router.push(location, onComplete?, onAbort?)
```

It is worth noting that you can access the router instance from within a Vue instance by typing $ router. As a result, you may execute this.$router.push.

Use router. Push to browse to a different URL. This technique adds an added item to the history stack, so that when the user hits the browser back button, they are returned to the prior URL.

Because this is the method called internally when you click a <router-link>, clicking a <router-link:to="..."> is equal to calling router.push (...).

Declarative	Programmatic
<router-link :to="...">	router.push(...)

The argument might be a string path or a location descriptor object. Examples:

```
// literal-string path
router.push('home')

// object
router.push({ path: 'home' })

// named-route
router.push({ name: 'user', params: { userId: '123' } })

// with the query, resulting in /register?plan=private
router.push({ path: 'register', query: { plan:
'private' } })
```

Note that if a path is specified, params are ignored, which is not the case with query, as seen in the preceding example. Instead, you must supply the route's name or explicitly define the entire path with any parameter:

```
const userId = '123'
router.push({ name: 'user', params: { userId } }) // ->
/user/123
```

```
router.push({ path: '/user/${userId}' }) // -> /user/123
// This will NOT work
router.push({ path: '/user', params: { userId } }) // ->
/user
```

The same rules apply to the router-link component's property.

Provide onComplete and onAbort callbacks to router.push or router in 2.2.0+. Replace with the second and third parameters. These callbacks will be triggered when the navigation is completed (after all async hooks have been handled) or aborted (navigated to the same or a different route before the current navigation has ended). In 3.1.0+ and later, you can skip the second and third arguments, as well as the router. Push/router. If Promises are supported, replace will return a promise instead.

Note: If the destination is the same as the current route and only the parameters change (e.g., /users/1 -> /users/2), you must use beforeRouteUpdate to react to changes (e.g., fetching the user information).

router.replace(location, onComplete?, onAbort?)
It functions similarly to router.push, with the exception that it navigates without pushing a new history item, as the name implies – instead, it replaces the existing entry.

Declarative	Programmatic
<router-link :to="..." replace>	router.replace(...)

router.go(n)
This function accepts a single integer as an argument that defines how many steps to travel forward or backward in the history stack, comparable to a window. history.go(n).

Example:

```
// go forward by one record, same as history.
forward()
router.go(1)

// go back by one record, same as history.back()
router.go(-1)

// go forward by three records
router.go(3)
```

```
// fails-silently if there are not that many
records.
router.go(-100)
router.go(100)
```

LAZY LOADING

What Is Lazy Loading in Vue.js?

Lazy loading is a design approach that postpones the initialization of components and objects until they are required. Lazy loading indicates that a target DOM element is loaded and becomes visible (when there is an intersection between two sections, based on a given threshold value) only when a user scrolls across a webpage.

To comprehend lazy loading, you must first comprehend eager loading. The default method for loading JavaScript code onto the DOM is eager loading. The import statement in Vue.js is used to introduce a component into the App. vue file. Lazy loading is a technique in which all scripts are not loaded on the DOM as soon as the program starts. Instead, they are only loaded when requested, resulting in a very minimal JavaScript bundle size upon initial load.

Vue.js handles component loading lazily with routes, so you may load components only when needed on the DOM via routes. This is accomplished by separating the components of each route into chunks distinct from the main chunk loaded during setup. This prevents the bundle size delivered to the DOM from getting excessively huge. To lazy-load route components, Vue.js utilizes the async component capability with webpack's code splitting feature.

Why Is Lazy Loading Significant?

The eager loading strategy makes the JS bundle quite onerous as your Vue. js project develops in size and complexity. This can be an issue for your end consumers, who may be using a mobile device or are not connected to a high-speed Internet connection.

Lazy loading ensures that your JavaScript bundle is given to the DOM components are listed in terms of hierarchy, from most important to least important. This method guarantees that you have complete control over the user's experience, including the initial wait period as resources are loaded into the DOM.

Vue.js Lazy Loading Example

To display lazy loading in Vue.js, we will use the Vue CLI to create an example Vue.js app and add routing during the configuration step.

We will also manually build a third route to demonstrate the procedure for developers who are unfamiliar with the Vue CLI. However, it is always recommended to utilize the Vue CLI because secondary routes are already set to be loaded lazily by default.

Starting a Vue.js Project

Open a terminal in a directory of your choosing and run the following command to create a new project:

```
vue create test_project
```

A follow-up questionnaire will look something like this:

```
? Please pick a preset: Manually select features
? Check the features needed for your project:
 ◉ Babel
 ○ TypeScript
 ○ Progressive Web App (PWA) Support
>◉ Router
 ○ Vuex
 ○ CSS Pre-processors
 ◉ Linter / Formatter
 ○ Unit Testing
 ○ E2E Testing
```

Make sure you use the spacebar to choose the router choice as shown above. Then, to minimize space, you may keep all the configurations in the package.json file. You will receive a success message after the project has been established. Change the location to the new project folder and execute the program in the development environment at this point:

```
cd test_project
npm run serve
```

Welcome to Your Vue.js App

For a guide and recipes on how to configure / customize this project,
check out the vue-cli documentation.

Welcome screen.

```
import Vue from 'vue'
import Router from 'vue-router'
import Home from './views/Home.vue'
import About from './views/About.vue'
Vue.use(Router)
export default new Router({
  routes: [
    {
      path: '/',
      name: 'home',
      component: Home
    },
    {
      path: '/about',
      name: 'about',
      component: About
    }
  ]
})
```

Because the Vue CLI allows lazy loading for secondary routes, such as the about component in our example, this may appear different for the about component part.

I Was Manually Adding a New Route

You now have two routes: a home route that leads to the home view and an about route that leads to the about view. Let us add a third view and then assign it to a course.

Make a new file in your views folder call extra.vue. After that, put the contents of the about.vue file into the extra.vue file. This is how it should look:

```
<template>
<div class="about">
<h1>This is an extra page</h1>
</div>
</template>
```

To add the route, open your router.js file and add the following code block to the routes array:

```
export default new router ({
  routes: [
```

```
    {
      path: '/',
      name: 'home',
      component: Home
    },
    {
      path: '/about',
      name: 'about',
      component: About
    },
    {

      path: '/extra',
      name: 'extra',
      component: Extra
    }
  ]
})
```

The last step in making it visible in the DOM is to add it to the main App .vue file through a router link.

Change the template section in your app.vue file to the code block below:

```
<template>
<div id="app">
<div id="nav">
<router-link to="/">Home</router-link> |
<router-link to="/about">About</router-link> |
<router-link to="/extra">Extra</router-link>
</div>
<router-view/>
</div>
</template>
```

How to Lazily Load Vue.js Components

Now that we have configured all the routes in our example Vue.js project, it is time to setup all your routes to be loaded lazily on request.

Open your router.js file and paste the following code block into it:

```
import Vue from 'vue'
import Router from 'vue-router.'
Vue.use(Router)
function lazyLoad(view){
  return() => import('@/views/${view}.vue')
}
```

```
export default new Router({
  mode: 'history',
  base: process.env.BASE_URL,
  routes: [
    {
      path: '/',
      name: 'home',
      component: lazyLoad('Home')
    },
    {
      path: '/about',
      name: 'about',
      component: lazyLoad('About')
    },
    {
      path: '/extra',
      name: 'extra',
      component: lazyLoad('extra')
    }
  ]
})
```

The following is a breakdown of what was done to make these views load more slowly.

Removing Import Statements

You might have spotted import statements for Vue.js, Router, Home, About, and other things at first. Because these statements are responsible for the eager loading of components, you must delete them when you change to the slow loading strategy.

lazyLoad Function

The Vue lazyLoad method was designed to tidy up the import statement. Every component would have a long-import statement if this function did not exist. You may just invoke the process and pass the path as args.

webpack Import Statement

The import statement that instructs webpack to load components asynchronously must be included in the routes section rather than the import section at the beginning of the script.

Rerun the program in development to test the loading strategy:

```
npm run serve
```

In your browser, navigate to http://localhost:8080/ and launch the developer tools. Select the JS tab from the network section.

The JavaScript chunks loaded on the DOM are divided into numbers, with the first (0.js) representing the home view, the second (1.js) representing the about view, which is only added to the DOM on click, and the third (2.js) representing the different view, which is also added to the DOM on request.

You can also test that the lazy loading worked by building up the application for production using the command:

```
npm run build
```

Webpack will represent these three chunks as separate independent and lazily loaded chunks.

Which Scripts Can You Load Lazily?

Of course, you write a lot of script code in Vue projects – after all, you are working with a lot of components (and context, hooks, etc.).

There are two types of code that can be loaded lazily in component-focused web projects like the ones you are creating with Vue:

- **Components:** Load component code (and any related code) only when a component is displayed on the screen.

- **Routes:** When a user accesses a route, just route component code (and all related code) is loaded.

How to Add Lazy Loading

Both are constructed in the same way: with async components.

Here is how to declare a component as "lazy-loaded":

```
{
  components: {
    'user-profile': () => import('./user-profile/
UserProfile');
  }
}
```

You use this lazy loaded component just like any other component:

```
<div v-if="someCondition">
  <user-profile></user-profile>
</div>
```

For routing, it is quite similar:

```
const router = new VueRouter({
  routes: [
    {
      path: '/user-profile',
      component: () => import('./user-profile/
UserProfile'),
    },
  ],
});
```

Vue and the underlying build process tool (e.g., Webpack) handle everything else; you do not need to do anything else.

Lazy loading, as the name implies, is the act of loading bits (chunks) of your program in a haphazard manner. In other words, you only load them when we need them. The technique of breaking the App into these lazily loaded portions is known as code splitting.

When a visitor views your website, you won't always need all of the code from your JavaScript bundle immediately away.

For example, we don't need to expend vital resources by loading the "My Page" portion of our website for first-time users. Modals, tooltips, and other sections and components that are not required on every page may also be included.

At best, downloading, parsing, and executing the full bundle everything on every page load is inefficient when just a few bits are required.

Lazy loading enables us to separate the bundle and deliver just the bits that are required, preventing users from spending time downloading and processing code that will not be utilized.

To examine how much JavaScript code is really utilized on our website; go to dev tools -> cmd+shift+p -> type coverage -> hit 'record.' We should now be able to observe how much of the downloaded code was really utilized.

Everything in red is unneeded on the current path and may be loaded lazily. If you are utilizing source maps, you may view which parts were not invoked by clicking on any file in this list. Even vuejs.org, as we can see, has a lot of space for development.

We were able to reduce the bundle size of Vue Storefront by 60% by lazily loading suitable components and libraries. That is the simplest technique to improve performance.

Okay, we know what lazy loading is and how beneficial it is. Now let us look at how we may leverage lazy loading in our Vue.js apps.

Dynamic Imports

With webpack dynamic imports, we may fast load specific components of our application in a lazy manner. Let us have a look at how they function and how they vary from standard imports.

If we import a JavaScript module in the conventional method, it will look like this:

```
// cat.js
const Cat = {
  meow: function () {
    console.log("Meowwwww!")
  }
}
export default Cat

// main.js
import Cat from './cat.js'
Cat.meow()
```

It will be added to the dependency graph as a node of a main.js and packed with it.

But what if we only require our Cat module in particular situations, for as in reaction to user interaction? This module should not be included in our first bundle because it is not required at all times. We need a method to inform our program when to download this piece of code.

This is when dynamic imports come in handy! Consider the following example:

```
// main.js
const getCat = () => import('./cat.js')
// later in the code as a response to some user interaction
like click or route change
getCat()
  .then({ meow } => meow())
```

Let us look at what occurred here quickly:

Instead of importing the Cat module directly, we constructed a method that returns the import() function. The content of the dynamically imported module will now be bundled into a separate file by webpack. The method that represents a dynamically imported module returns a Promise that gives us access to the module's exported members while it is resolved.

We may then download this optional portion as needed in the future, for example, because of specific user interactions (like route change or click).

By using a dynamic import, we isolate the specified node (in this example, Cat) that will be added to the dependency tree and download this portion when we determine it is required (which implies that we are also cutting off imported modules inside Cat.js).

Let us look at another example to further understand this technique. Assume we have a tiny webstore with four files:

- main.js as our main bundle

- product.js for scripts on the product page

- productGallery.js for product gallery on the product page

- category.js for hands in the category page

Without going into too much depth, let us look at how those files are dispersed across the application:

```
// category.js
const category = {
  init () { ... }
}
export default category
```

```
// product.js
import gallery from ('./productGallery.js')

const product = {
 init () { ... }
}
export default product

// main.js
const getProduct = () => import('./product.js')
const getCategory = () => import('./category.js')

if (route === "/product") {
 getProduct()
   .then({init} => init()) // run scripts for product
page
}
if (route === "/category") {
 getCategory()
   .then({init} => init()) // run scripts for category
page
}
```

Depending on the current path, we dynamically import either the product or category modules and then perform the init method exposed by both.

Knowing how dynamic imports work, we know that product and category will end up in distinct bundles, but what about the productGallery module, which was not dynamically imported? As we know, by dynamically importing the module, we are removing a portion of the dependency network. Everything imported within this component will be combined; therefore, productGallery will be included in the same bundle as the product module.

In other words, we are simply adding a new entry point to the dependency graph.

Lazy Loading Vue Components

We now understand what lazy loading is and why we require it. It is time to look at how we can use it in our Vue apps.

The good news is that it is incredibly simple, and we can load the complete Single File Component, including its CSS and HTML, using the same syntax as before.

```
const lazyComponent = () => import('Component.vue')
```

...and that is all you need! The component will now only be downloaded when it is requested. The following are the most frequent methods for invoking dynamic loading of a Vue component:

- function with the import is invoked

```
const lazyComponent = () => import('Component.
vue')
lazyComponent()
```

- The rendering of a component is requested.

```
<template>
  <div>
    <lazy-component />
  </div>
</template>

<script>
const lazyComponent = () => import('Component.vue')
export default {
  components: { lazyComponent }
}

// Another syntax
export default {
  components: {
    lazyComponent: () => import('Component.vue')
  }
}
</script>
```

Please keep in mind that the lazyComponent method is only called when the component is requested to render in a template. For instance, consider the following code:

```
<lazy-component v-if="false" />
```

When the v-if value switches to true, the component will not be loaded until it is required in the DOM.

When using a bundler to develop apps, the JavaScript bundle might get quite huge, affecting page load time. It would more efficient if we could divide the components of each route into discrete chunks and only load them when route is visited.

It is a simple task to lazy-load route components using Vue's async component feature (opens new window) and webpack's code splitting functionality (opens new window).

To begin, an async component is a factory function that returns a Promise (which should resolve to the component itself):

```
const Foo = () =>
  Promise.resolve({
    /* component definition */
  })
```

Second, we may utilize the dynamic import (opens new window) terminology in webpack 2 to identify a code-split point:

```
import('./Foo.vue') // returns a Promise
```

Combining the two, this is how you construct an async component that will be code-split automatically by webpack:

```
const Foo = () => import('./Foo.vue')
```

Nothing must be changed in the route configuration; simply use Foo as usual:

```
const router = new VueRouter({
  routes: [{ path: '/foo', component: Foo }]
})
```

Grouping Components in the Same Chunk

We may wish to group all the components contained under the same route into the same async chunk at times. To do this, we must utilize named chunks (opens new window) by specifying a chunk name using comment syntax (webpack > 2.4 required):

```
const Foo = () => import(/* webpackChunkName: "group-foo" */ './Foo.vue')
const Bar = () => import(/* webpackChunkName: "group-foo" */ './Bar.vue')
const Baz = () => import(/* webpackChunkName: "group-foo" */ './Baz.vue')
```

Any async module with the same chunk name will be grouped into the same async chunk by webpack.

CONCLUSION

We discussed programmatic navigation and lazy loading in this chapter, including what they are and how they are utilized. We will learn about sophisticated context API in the next chapter.

CHAPTER 7

Advanced API Concepts

IN THIS CHAPTER

> Context API

In Chapter 6, we learned about programmatic navigation and lazy loading, what they are, and how they are used. In this chapter, we will learn about advanced Context API.

CONTEXT API

The React Context API allows a React project to generate global variables that may effectively pass around. This is an alternative to "prop drilling," in which props are passed from grandparent to kid to parent, and so on. "Context is also advertised as a simpler, lighter approach to handle Redux state." ("React – Context API – DEV Community").

Context API is a new feature introduced in React 16.3 that allows you to easily and lightweight communicate state across the entire project (or part of it).

Will Context API Replace Redux?

Redux is fantastic and ideally suited to the requirement for state management. It met this demand so effectively that it became widely accepted that you cannot call oneself a "real" React developer if you do not know your

DOI: 10.1201/9781003310464-7

way around Redux. However, Redux has drawbacks, which is why it is crucial to understand what Context API provides that Redux does not:

- **Simplicity:** When individuals use Redux, they tend to maintain all their state in Redux, which poses two issues:

  1. **Overhead:** Why should I create/update three files to introduce a single minor feature?

  2. One of the most notable benefits of React's one-way data binding is its simplicity – a component provides state to its descendants. When we utilize Redux, it is taken away from us.

- Using the Context API, we may establish several unconnected contexts (stores) and utilize each in its rightful location inside the program.

Important Note

Redux is only an idea. Assume you are comfortable with reducers and actions and do not find them to be a hindrance. In that situation, as Redux's inventor Dan Abramov highlighted in his medium piece about whether Redux is always necessary, you may also design reducers and actions that cover Context API as the store.

How Do I Utilize the Context API?

You may be thinking to yourself: "So far, I'm satisfied. How do I include Context API into my app?" First, be certain that you require it. People will sometimes utilize shared state across nested components instead than just giving them as props. And if you do require it, you should do the following steps:

1. Make a folder called contexts inside your app's root (optional). only a convention).

2. Make a file called <your context name>Context.js, for example, userContext.js.

3. Import and construct a context as follows:

```
import React, { createContext } from "react";
const UserContext = createContext();
```

4. Create a component named Provider that will cover the provider, e.g., UserProvider.

5. A React Hooks example:

```
const UserProvider = ({ children }) => {
  const [name, setName] = useState("Johny Doe");
  const [age, setAge] = useState(1);
  const happyBirthday = () => setAge(age + 1);
  return (
    <UserContext.Provider value={{ name, age,
happyBirthday }}>
      {children}
    </UserContext.Provider>
  );
};
```

6. Create a higher-order component named with, for example, with-User, to consume the context.

7. Example using React Hooks:

```
const withUser = (Child) => (props) => (
  <UserContext.Consumer>
    { (context) => <Child {...props} {...context} />}
    {/* Another option is: {context => <Child {...
props} context={context}/>}*/}
  </UserContext.Consumer>
);
```

The difference between the two options above is whether you want the context to be a single nested property by this name, or whether you want it to explode to its properties (which is more convenient).

8. Finally export.

```
export { UserProvider, withUser };
```

9. And use them however you like.

10. For instance:

```
ReactDOM.render(
  <UserProvider>
    <App />
  </UserProvider>,
  document.getElementById("root")
);
export default withUser(LoginForm);
```

Learn How the React Context API Works and when to Utilize It to Avoid Prop-Drilling in Your Application

One of the nicest things about React is that we have a plethora of options for solving specific situations. We also have a few more forms of libraries, a slew of CSS libraries, and, for the most important portion of React, a slew of other libraries related to state data concerns in React.

Identifying when to utilize a specific library in our project is a talent that we get through practice. Particularly with React, where there are so many libraries to pick from, we may get up installing and utilizing libraries that we do not require.

Context API is a React API that may handle a variety of problems related to state management and how state is delivered to components in modern projects. Rather than installing a state management library in your project, which can reduce project performance and increase bundle size, you may just utilize Context API and be OK.

Let us go through what the Context API is, what issues it solves, and how to use it.

Why Context API?

One of React's principles is to divide your application into components for reusability. So we have a few different components in a small React application. As our application expands, these components might become large and unmanageable, so we need to split them down into smaller bits.

That is one of React's finest ideas: you can design several components and have a maintained and succinct application without needing to make a super-colossal component to deal with your entire application.

After breaking components down into smaller components for the sake of maintainability, these little components may now require certain data to operate normally. If these little components require data to function, data must be sent from the parent component to the child component using props. This is where we may slow down our application and cause problems with development.

Assume we have a component named Notes that oversees rendering a lot of notes.

```
const Notes = () => {
  const [notes] = useState([
    {
      title: "First note",
      description: "This is first note",
      done: false
    }
  ]);
  return (
    <div>
    <h1>Notes</h1>
      {notes.map(note => {
        return (
        <div>
          <h1>{note.title}</h1>
          <h3>{note.description}</h3>
          <p>{note.done?  "done!"  :  "not done!"}</p>
        </div>
        );
      })}
    </div>
  );
};
```

We can see from this code that we can divide this component down into smaller components, making our code clearer and more manageable. For example, we might construct a Note component and then nest three additional components within it: Title, Description, and Done.

```
const Notes = () => {
  const [notes] = estate([
    {
      title: "First note",
      description: "This is first note",
      done: false
    }
  ]);
```

```
  return (
    <div>
      <h1>Notes</h1>
      {notes.map(({ title, description, done }) => {
        return <Note title={title}
description={description} done={done} />;
      })}
    </div>
  );
};

const Note = ({ title, description, done }) => {
  return (
    <div>
      <Title title={title} />
      <Description description={description} />
      <Done done={done} />
    </div>
  );
};

const Title = ({ title }) => {
  return <h1>{title}</h1>;
};

const Description = ({ description }) => {
  return <h3>{description}</h3>;
};

const Description = ({ description }) => {
  return <h3>{description}</h3>;
};
```

We now have a few components, and our sample application's reusability and maintainability have improved. However, if this application increases in size and we feel the need to divide these components down into smaller components in the future, we may have a problem.

Passing data via props repeatedly might cause issues for your application. You may provide more support than necessary at times, or you may neglect to send necessary props, rename props via the components without realizing it, and so on. Assume you are providing data from the parent component to a fourth- or fifth-level component using props. In such instance, you are not reusing and producing maintainable code, which may jeopardize the future of your program.

This is referred to as "prop-drilling." In the medium to long term, this might annoy and slow down your development – repeatedly giving props to your components will cause future difficulties in your application.

That is one of the primary issues that Context API was created to address for us.

Context API

The Context API may be used to communicate data with different components without having to explicitly feed data through props. The Context API, for example, is suited for the following use cases: theming, user language, authentication, and so on.

createContext

To begin using the Context API, we must first build a context using React's createContext method.

```
const NotesContext = createContext([]);
```

The createContext method takes an initial value; however, it is not needed.

After you have created your context, it now has two React components: Provider and Consumer.

Provider

The Provider component will be used to encapsulate all the components that will have access to our context.

```
<NotesContext.Provider value={this.state.notes}>
...
</Notes.Provider>
```

The Provider component is given a prop named value, which can be accessed by all the components wrapped inside it, and it oversees giving access to the context data.

Consumer

After you have wrapped all the components that will need access to the context in the Provider component, you must specify which component will consume that data.

A React component can subscribe to context changes using the Consumer component. A render prop is used by the component to make the data available.

```
<NotesContext.Consumer>
   {values => <h1>{value</h1>}
</Notes.Consumer>
```

useContext

You may have been using React Hooks for some time now, but if you do not know what they are or how they operate, let me explain them to you briefly:

- React Hooks enable us to handle state data within functional components; we no longer need to develop class components to manage state data.
- React has several built-in hooks like as estate, useCallback, useEffect, and so on. But the one we will be discussing and learning more about here is the useContext hook.

We may connect to and consume a context using the useContext hook. The useContext hook takes a single parameter, which is the context to which you wish to get access.

```
const notes = useContext(NotesContext);
```

The useContext component is far superior than the Consumer component in terms of readability and maintainability, we can quickly grasp what is going on and improve the overall maintainability of our application.

Now, let us make an example using the Context API and the hook to show how it works in practice. We will create a basic application to determine whether the user is authorized or not.

We will name the file context.js. Within that file, we will construct our context and provider, import the estate and useContext hooks from React, and establish our context, which we will call AuthContext. For the time being, the initial value of our AuthContext will be undefined.

```
import React, { estate, useContext } from "react";
const AuthContext = React.createContext(undefined);
```

We will develop a functional component named AuthProvider, which will accept children as props. Within this component, we will render more items and handle the state data that we want to exchange with the other components.

```
const AuthProvider = ({ children }) => {
...
};
```

First, we will construct our auth state. This will be a basic Boolean state used to determine whether or not the user is authorized. In addition, we will write a method named handleAuth that will be in charge of changing our auth state.

```
const [auth, setAuth] = useState(false);
const handleAuth = () => {
  setAuth(!auth);
};
```

Because the Provider does not accept array values, we will build an array named data that contains our auth state and our handleAuth method. This information will pass as a value to our AuthContextProvider.

```
const AuthProvider = ({ children }) => {
  const [auth, setAuth] = useState(false);
  const handleAuth = () => {
    setAuth(!auth);
  };
  const data = [auth, handleAuth];
  return <AuthContext.Provider value={data}>{children}
</AuthContext.Provider>;
};
```

Now, within our context.js file, we will add a simple hook component named useAuth, which will be used to consume our context. If we try to utilize this component outside of our Provider, it will crash.

```
const useAuth = () => {
  const context = useContext(AuthContext);
  if (context === undefined) {
```

```
    throw new Error("useAuth can only use inside
AuthProvider");
  }
  return context;
};
```

Then, toward the conclusion of our function, we'll export and useAuth our AuthProvider.

Now, in our index.js component, we must import the AuthProvider component and wrap the components that we want to allow context access within this provider. ("Understand React Context API – Telerik Blogs")

```
import { AuthProvider } from "./context";
ReactDOM.render(
  <React.StrictMode>
  <AuthProvider>
  <App />
  </AuthProvider>
  </React.StrictMode>,
  rootElement
);
```

Next, we will handle our context data within our App.js file. To begin, we must import the useAuth hook we developed and obtain the auth and handleAuth from useAuth.

Let us make a button that will call the handleAuth method every time it is clicked. Let us also verify if the auth value changes as we click the button using a ternary rendering of a basic h1.

```
import { useAuth } from "./context";
const App = () => {
  const [auth, handleAuth] = useAuth(useAuth);
  return (
    <div>
      <h3>Is authenticated?</h3>
      <h1>{auth === false?  "Not authenticated" :
"Authenticated"}  </h1>
      <button onClick={handleAuth}>Change auth</
button>
    </div>
  );
};
```

We now have a simple application that makes use of the Context API. It is worth noting that we do not need to transfer any props from parent to child components.

In some instances, such as authentication, the Context API may be useful in identifying whether or not the user is authenticated in a number of unrelated components.

React's Context API and Provide/Inject in Vue

In a complicated app, you will frequently find circumstances in which you must provide many props from your parent component to a deeply nested child component. When confronted with such circumstances, DI is an especially useful tool.

Redux/Vuex is a popular dependency injection technology in the front-end realm. Along with DI, they solve several additional issues, such as predictable state transitions and those listed below.

Although a single store solves many difficulties, it has certain limits, which are as follows:

1. When you have a lot of features in your app, you want each one to have a unique context (store). You do not want one element of your app to interfere with another.

2. As a plugin developer, you do not want to erase the user's plugin-specific items from the user's store.

3. When you have a component linked to the shop, you want numerous instances of that component on your page. For example, if you have a form linked to the store, you need 2–3 forms on the same page.

React 16.3 debuted the context API, which quickly gained popularity. It was not anything out of the box that was not previously there, but better documentation and a concise API made it easier for developers to utilize DI and made it more accessible.

We are creating a form (in a later application) with numerous nested components, and we can have several form components on the page. As a result, in this scenario, all Form components cannot share a single store. We also do not want to destroy the user's state because we want to make this component open-source. Finally, if we utilize the primary Vuex store, the end-user will have to manually register it, making the plugin difficult to integrate.

Surprisingly, Vue.js provides a wonderful API (supply and inject) that is discussed below to assist you in creating a Context API-like API. Here is how I did it.

Please keep in mind that I have deleted our plugin-specific code for obvious reasons.

Plugin/core/util/store-template.js

```
export const state = () => ({
   data: {},
   errors: []
})
export const mutations = {
}
export const actions = {
}
```

This is the location of my store file. This file is stored within the plugin, and it contains all the plugin-related code for the store.

Plugin/core/index.vue

```
<template>
    <div class="Form">
        <!-- <NestedComponent /> -->
    </div>
</template>

<script>
import { storeTemplate } from "./core/util";
import Vuex from "vuex";
export default {
    name: "Form",
    props: {
        ischemia: {
            type: Object,
            required: true
        },
        schema: {
            type: Object,
            required: true
        },
```

```
        data: {
            type: Object
        },
        renderers: {
            type: Array
        }
    },
    data() {
        return {
            iStore: new Vuex.Store({
                state: storeTemplate.state,
                mutations: storeTemplate.mutations,
                actions: storeTemplate.actions
            })
        };
    },
    provide: function() {
        return {
            iStore: this.iStore
        };
    },
    created() {
        this.iStore.dispatch("initForm", {
            uiSchema: this.uiSchema,
            renderers: this.renderers,
            schema: this.schema,
            data: this.data
        });
        this.iStore.subscribe((mutation, state) => {
            if (mutation.type == "updateData") {
                this.$emit("onDataChanged", state.data);
            }
        });
    },
    computed: {}
};
</script>

<style lang="scss">
    .Form {
        width: 100%;
        height: 100%;
    }
</style>
```

This is the plugin's primary file, and it is executed anytime the user renders the form component in his component. As shown in the data hook, I am creating a new store instance and assigning it to the iStore key in the supplying function.

Plugin/components/nested-component.vue

```
<template>
        <div>
                        <div>Nested form component</div>
        </div>
</template>

<script>
export { ReviewLayoutTester };
export default {
        props: {},
        inject: ["iStore"],
        mounted() {
                        console.log(this.iStore.state.
data);
        }
};
</script>

<style>
</style>
```

You can just inject iStore into any of the child nested components and begin utilizing it.

We do not need to educate the user about anything internal because all the Form components can handle own stores. Furthermore, all plugin-specific code is managed in a specific location within the plugin.

Many React and Vue libraries make use of DI. I liked the Material-with-styles UI approach when I first started working with React. DI might be difficult to think about and apply at times. However, by learning these approaches, you will not only be able to produce more maintainable code, but you will also be able to quickly understand and debug libraries, making you a better developer in general.

Assume you are developing an accordion component that you would like to make available to the public via an npm package. You want the accordion's user to be able to use the element in a highly flexible way by building many components together.

Assume the following is your ideal API:

```
<Accordion>
    <AccordionItem>
        <AccordionHeader>Header content</
AccordionHeader>
        <AccordionPanel>Panel content</AccordionPanel>
    </AccordionItem>
</Accordion>
```

AccordionItem contains each component of the accordion that may be extended or collapsed, AccordionHeader is where the user clicks to expand or collapse, and AccordionPanel contains the content to be shown or concealed.

Each AccordionItem must keep some state, whether it is expanded or not. However, AccordionHeader will also want access to this value to display the relevant toggle button. AccordionPanel may also require access to this because it is the item that is expanded and collapsed.

One option is to provide the enlarged value to the user via render properties and make sure your documentation informs them that they must send that down to the header and panel components.

```
<Accordion>
    <AccordionItem render={({expanded}) => (
        <AccordionHeader expanded={expanded}>
            Header content
        </AccordionHeader>
        <AccordionPanel expanded={expanded}>
            Panel content
        </AccordionPanel>
    )}
    />
</Accordion>
```

While this may appear to be a reasonable approach, it is not ideal that the Consumer of our component must be concerned with the component's internals. The fact that AccordionHeader and AccordionPanel require access to the extended state should not be a source of concern for our user.

It should also note that, while this is a simple example, your component may be significantly more complicated, with numerous levels of nested components, in which case prop drilling could become time consuming.

Using React's Context API

For situations like these, there is a better solution: React's Context API. We can utilize the Context API to construct some state and supply it where it is needed behind the scenes, removing this worry from our public-facing API.

To begin, we will establish a context and determine its shape. To begin, we will use an expanded value and a toggleExpansion function. This context is defined as being especially relevant to our accordion item:

```
const AccordionItemContext = React.createContext({
    expanded: false,
    toggleExpansion: () => {}
});
```

Now, under our AccordionItem component, we will specify the expanded and toggleExpansion values and pass them into the Provider component's value.

```
class AccordionItem extends React.Component {
    constructor (props) {
        super(props)

        this.toggleExpansion = () => {
            this.setState({ expanded: !this.state.
expanded })
        }

        this.state = {
            expanded: false,
            toggleExpansion: this.toggleExpansion
        }
    }

    render () {
        return (
            <AccordionItemContext.Provider
value={this.state}>
                <div className="accordion-item">
```

```
                {this.props.children}
            </div>
        </AccordionItemContext.Provider>
        )
    }
}
```

One-half of the Context equation is the Provider. The Consumer is the other side of the equation. As we will see shortly, the Provider enables the Consumer to subscribe to context changes.

Next, we must configure AccordionHeader and AccordionPanel as context consumers:

```
const AccordionHeader = (props) => {
    return (
        <AccordionItemContext.Consumer>
            {({ expanded, toggleExpansion }) => (
                <h2 className="accordion-header">
                    <button onClick={toggleExpansion}>
                        { expanded?  '▼' : '►' }
                        { props.children }
                    </button>
                </h2>
            )}
        </AccordionItemContext.Consumer>
    )
}
```

As a child, the Consumer component requires a function. This function will be sent the context value, which will be destructed into expanded and toggleExpansion. Our component may now use these data in its template.

Similarly, we will use Consumer to grant AccordionPanel access to the context value:

```
const AccordionPanel = (props) => {
    return (
        <AccordionItemContext.Consumer>
            {({ expanded }) => <div
className={"accordion-panel " + (expanded?  'expanded'
: '')}>{props.children}</div>}
        </AccordionItemContext.Consumer>
    )
}
```

Now we can truly create our perfect API for the accordion component. Our component's users will not have to worry about sending state up or down the component tree. They are unaware of the internals of the components:

```
<Accordion>
    <AccordionItem>
        <AccordionHeader>Header content</
AccordionHeader>
        <AccordionPanel>Panel content</
AccordionPanel>
    </AccordionItem>
</Accordion>
```

Provide/Inject in Vue

Vue has a tool called provide/inject that is comparable to React's Context API. We will utilize the supply method on our accordion-item Vue component to do so:

```
Vue.component('accordion-item', {
    data () {
        return {
            sharedState: {
                expanded: false
            }
        }
    },

    provide () {
        return {
            accordionItemState: this.sharedState
        }
    },

    render (createElement) {
        return createElement(
            'div',
            { class: 'accordion-item' },
            this.$slots.default
        )
    }
})
```

We return an object from providing () that contains the state we want to provide to other elements. It is worth noting that we send an object to accordionItemState rather than simply passing the <code">expanded value. To be reactive, supply must pass an object.

It should be noticed that we are generating this component with a render function, which is not essential to use provide/inject.

We will now inject this state into our child components. We will just utilize the inject property, which accepts an array of strings matching to the object's properties defined in give.

```
Vue.component('accordion-header', {
    inject: ['accordionItemState'],

    template: '
        <h2 class="accordion-header">
            <button @click="accordionItemState.
expanded = !accordionItemState.expanded">
                {{ accordionItemState.expanded?  '▼' :
'►' }}
                <slot></slot>
            </button>
        </h2>
        '
})
```

We can access those values in our template after we add the property name in inject.

```
Vue.component('accordion-panel', {
    inject: ['accordionItemState'],

    template: '
        <div class="accordion-panel" :class="{
expanded: accordionItemState.expanded }">
            <slot></slot>
        </div>
        '
})
```

Use with Caution

It is worth remembering that you should only send down props implicitly when it makes sense. Excessive usage of this might hide the true functionality of your components and confuse other developers who may be working on your project.

A packed and distributed component library for use in other applications is a suitable use case since the internal attributes of the components do not need to be disclosed to the end user.

Through implicit state sharing, React's Context API and Vue's provide/inject functionality enable this.

Complete Visibility into Production React Apps

Debugging React apps may be challenging, especially when users encounter bugs that are difficult to recreate. If you want to monitor and track Redux state, automatically uncover JavaScript bugs, and measure slow network queries and component load time, try LogRocket.

LogRocket functions similar to a DVR for web apps, capturing everything that occurs on your React project. Instead of speculating on why issues arise, you may collect and report on the condition of your application at the time an issue occurred. LogRocket also monitors the performance of your app, delivering data like as client CPU load, client memory consumption, and more.

The LogRocket Redux middleware package provides more visibility into your user sessions. LogRocket records all Redux store activities and states.

When working with the Vue 3 Composition API, there are several new ways to access component functionality. In this section, we'll look at the setup function's context argument.

These adjustments are required since the Composition API does not have the same reference to this as the Options API.

We could use the Options API to use console.log(this) in any of the options to acquire a reference to the component itself, allowing us access to its props, computed properties, data, and more.

```
export default {
  props: {
    Lastname: String,
  },
  data() {
    return {
      name: "hello",
    };
  },
  created() {
```

```
    console.log(this.lastNameModifiers); // props are
on 'this'
    console.log(this.name); // data is on 'this'
    this.createdMethod(); // methods are on 'this'
  },
  methods: {
    createdMethod() {
      console.log("created");
    },
  },
};
```

Vue 3, on the other hand, allows us to use the Composition API, where all our code is contained within a setup function. This implies that we define our reactive data, methods, and calculated properties in setup.

```
import { ref } from "vue";
export default {
  props: {
    Lastname: String,
  },
  setup() {
    // How do we get access to props if we do not have
this?
    const createdMethod = () => {
      console.log("created");
    };
    const name = ref("hello");

    createdMethod();
    return {
      createdMethod,
      name,
    };
  },
};
```

Setup occurs prior to the creation of our component instance. Because our setup property defines everything for our component, this no longer contains a reference to the element itself.

So How Do We Access Component Properties?

The Composition API provides us with additional ways to retrieve critical component information such as props and slots.

This is feasible because our setup method accepts two attributes that allow us to access component properties: props and context. props contain declared props in our component. A context is a JavaScript object that exposes three attributes.

These three characteristics are as follows:

1. **Context.attracts:** the non-prop attributes given to our component.

2. **Context.slots:** an object containing all the render methods for our template slots.

3. **Context.emit:** the technique through which our component communicates events.

Let's take a deeper look at each of these.

context.attrs

Again, context.attrs holds all the non-prop attributes that have been passed to our component.

What exactly does this mean?

Any element property we add that is not stated in our props will be available within context.attrs when we utilize our component.

Assume we have a custom component that accepts a value prop.

```
export default {
  props: {
    value: String,
  },
  setup(props, context) {
    console.log(context.attrs);
  },
};
```

Then we pass it numerous characteristics in a parent component.

```
<template>
  <custom-component
    :value="value"
```

```
      test="hi"
      @close="close"
    />
</template>
```

As you can see, it includes everything except our stated props. Event listeners and HTML attributes are examples of this.

One thing to keep in mind is that attrs is not reactive. That is, if we wish to implement side effects in response to attrs values changing, we should instead utilize the onUpdated lifecycle hook.

context.slots

Next, consider the context. Slots are a little perplexing, so let us go over an example of why they are beneficial.

In a word, context. Slots provide us with access to the render method of each slot. This is important when we are not utilizing template code and are developing our own unique render method.

Vue suggests utilizing templates in most circumstances; however, if you genuinely want to get into the full power of JavaScript, we can write our own render functions.

An excellent time to utilize a custom render method, according to the Vue instructions, is when we are developing a component that renders a slot value with a different level heading depending on the value of a prop.

```
<template>
  <div>
    <h1 v-if="level == 1">
      <slot />
    </h1>
    <h2 v-if="level == 2">
      <slot />
    </h2>
    <h3 v-if="level == 3">
      <slot />
    </h3>
    <h4 v-if="level == 4">
      <slot />
    </h4>
    <h5 v-if="level == 5">
      <slot />
    </h5>
```

```
      <h6 v-if="level == 6">
        <slot />
      </h6>
    </div>
  </template>
  <script>
    export default {
        props: {
            level: Number,
        },
    }
  </script>
```

For all six heading options, we use v-if and v-else-if conditionals in this code. And, as you can see, there is a lot of identical codes, making the page appear excessively cluttered.

Instead, we might construct our heading programmatically by using the render method. This is what the Composition API setup method looks like.

```
import { h } from "vue";
export default {
  props: {
    level: Number,
  },
  setup(props, context) {
    console.log("here");
    return () =>
      h(
        "h" + props.level,
        {} // props and attributes: OPTIONAL
        /* MISSING! this is where children go, for us
our slot */
      );
  },
};
```

However, how can we get our slots to render?

That is where context comes into play. Slot comes into play.

By providing us access to the render function of each slot. Each slot is accessible by its name, and because we did not specifically identify our slot, it is named default.

```
import { h } from "vue";
export default {
  props: {
    level: Number,
  },
  setup(props, context) {
    console.log("here");
    return () =>
      h(
        "h" + props.level,
        {}, // props and attributes: OPTIONAL
        context.slots.default() /* Rendering default
slot */
      );
  },
};
```

Now, if we run this with a basic parent component like this, we will see what happens.

```
<template>
    <child-component :level="1">
      Hello Everyone
    </child-component>
</template>
```

context.emit

Finally, consider the context. emit takes the place of this.$emit as our method of emitting events from our component.

This is handy for transmitting any type of event to a parent component, with or without data.

Assume we want to make an X button that generates a close event.

```
<template>
  <div>
    <button @click="closeModal">X</button>
  </div>
</template>
<script>
  export default {
      setup (props, context) {
        const closeModal = () => {
```

```
        context.emit('close' /* can pass payload
here */)
      }
      return {
        closeModal
      }
    }
  }
</script>
```

Then, using the von directive, we can listen for this closure event within our parent component.

```
<modal-component @close="handleClose" />
```

What do we not have access to during setup?

So far, we have seen how the Composition API provides us with access to four diverse types of properties: props, attrs, slots, and emit.

However, because setup occurs before our component instance is formed, we will not have access to the following three component properties:

- data

- computed

- methods

These are properties that we define within setup, but there is no built-in mechanism to access a list of all data properties, for example.

CONCLUSION

This chapter taught us about Context APIs, what they are, and how to utilize them. In the following chapter, we will learn about testing, nock, and Vue.js-testing-library.

CHAPTER 8

Vue Testing Library

IN THIS CHAPTER

➢ NOCK

➢ Vue.js-testing-library

We learned about Context API, including what they are and how they are utilized, in Chapter 7. This chapter will teach us about testing, Nock, and the Vue.js-testing-library.

NOCK

Nock is a Node.js server mocking and expectations library.

Nock may use to isolate and test modules that perform HTTP requests.

For example, if a module sends HTTP queries to a CouchDB server or the Amazon API, you may isolate that module and test it separately.

How Does It Work?

Nock works by altering the HTTP.request method in Node. It also overrides HTTP.ClientRequest to enable modules that utilize it directly.

We shall check:

• Why mock HTTP requests during testing?

• What is Nock?

• Code examples of the both Nock and Nock.back.

DOI: 10.1201/9781003310464-8

Why Perform Mock HTTP Requests during Testing?

Maintaining test coverage and writing reliable tests may be difficult when dealing with code that relies on external services. For a number of reasons, tests that perform real HTTP queries to external services might be error-prone. For example, the precise data delivered varies with each request, network connectivity issues, or even rate limitation.

Unless the test is expressly meant to verify the availability, response speed, or data form of an external service, it should not fail due to an external reliance.

Intercepting and regulating the behavior of external HTTP requests restores the trustworthiness of our tests. This is when Nock enters.

What Is Nock?

- Nock is a Node.js HTTP server mocking and expectations library.

- Nock may use to test modules that perform HTTP requests.

- Nock works by altering the HTTP.request method in Node. It also overrides HTTP.ClientRequest to accommodate modules that utilize it directly.

By intercepting external HTTP queries and allowing us to either send bespoke replies to test different situations or save accurate results as "fixtures," canned data that will return trustworthy responses, Nock helps us to avoid the mentioned problems.

Using prepared data has drawbacks, since it might get stale if not renewed regularly. Without explicit extra tests or pinned API versioning, a change in the form of the data delivered by an API may go undetected. The developer's responsibility is to ensure that preventative measures are in place.

In our end-to-end testing, we see an example from my present company. These make use of Nock fixtures since they would occasionally fail due to timeouts when executed as part of our continuous delivery process. When a developer performs these tests locally, the fixtures are immediately removed and regenerated, ensuring that they are always up to date.

Currently, Nock is used in two ways:

- Nock is used to mock particular replies defined by the developer.

- Nock.back is used for recording, saving, and reusing live answers.

Both can be found in individual tests. If both are used in the same test file, the nock.back mode must be set and reset explicitly before and after usage. We'll go through this in further detail later.

Let's create a project, add Nock, and then compare Nock to Nock. I'm back with some more code examples.

Adding Nock

This example project will build. It includes several simple methods that call a random user generating API, making it ideal for testing with Nock. It employs Jest as a test runner and assertion generator.

In the example to be tested, three functions are available: obtaining a random user, getting a random user of a certain nationality, and getting a random user but falling back to default settings if failed. Here's an example:

```
const getRandomUserOfNationality = n =>
  fetch('https://randomuser.me/api/?nat=${n}')
    .then(throwNon200)
    .then(res => res.json())
    .catch(e => console.log(e));
```

We were using Nock at the time. A nock.js auxiliary file was utilized back then, which we shall look into later.

Using 'nock'

This is nicely explained in the Nock docs. There are several possibilities for specifying the request modification, whether in the matched request or the answer provided. The response received following a successful request and producing a 500 response to test a function's fallback options are two instances.

All that would need to add to existing test file to start using Nock is const nock = require('nock'); / import nock from 'nock';.

In the first test, we match the hostname and path with a string and specify a reply code and message. The assertion is subsequently added to our function call's Promise chain. When the incoming request from get random user() matches the Nock interceptor we just configured, the reply we defined is returned.

```
it('should return a user', () => {

  nock('https://randomuser.me')
```

```
.get('/api/')
.reply(200, {
  results: [{ name: 'Dominic' }],
}); return query
.getRandomUser()
.then(res => res.results[0].name)
.then(res => expect(res).toEqual('Dominic'));});
```

Similarly, we mimic a call with a specified nationality, but this time we match the hostname and path using a RegExp.

```
it('should return a user of set nationality', () =>
{ nock(/random/)
  .get(/nat=gb/)
  .reply(200, {
    results: [{ nat: 'GB' }],
  }); return query
  .getRandomUserOfNationality('gb')
  .then(res => res.results[0].nat)
  .then(res => expect(res).toEqual('GB'));});
```

It's worth noting that we're using afterAll(Nock.restore) and afterEach (Nock.cleanAll) to ensure that interceptors don't conflict with one another.

Finally, we run a 500 response test. For this, we developed a new method that returns a default value if the API request does not provide a response. Before verifying the function's output, we use Nock to intercept the request and simulate a 500 response.

```
it('should return a default user on 500', () => {
nock(/randomuser/)
  .get(/api/)
  .reply(500); return query
  .getRandomUserGuarded()
  .then(res => expect(res).toMatchObject(defaultU
ser));});
```

It's really handy to be able to mimic non-200 response codes, connection delays, and socket timeouts.

Using 'nock.back'

The function nock.back is used not only to intercept an HTTP request, but also to record the actual response for further usage. This stored response is known as a "fixture."

If the identified fixture is present in record mode, it will be used instead of live calls; otherwise, a fixture will be established for future calls.

Although just one HTTP request is performed per test in our sample project, nock.back fixtures are capable of logging all outgoing calls. This is especially handy when testing a complicated component that contacts several services, or when performing end-to-end testing, when a variety of calls might be made. The key benefit of utilizing fixtures is that they are quick to access once established, eliminating the possibility of time-outs. Because they are using genuine data, mimicking the data structure is unnecessary, and any changes can be detected.

As previously stated, it is critical to remove and refresh fixtures on a regular basis to prevent them from becoming stale.

A current "feature" of nock.back is that it can interfere with ordinary nock interceptors when used in the same test file, without any nock is utilized.

Back tests are bookended every test in the following manner:

```
nock.back.setMode('record');// your testnock.back.
setMode('wild');
```

This guarantees that any subsequent tests do not mistakenly utilize the fixtures that were just prepared. If this is not done, then, for example, the 500 answer in our earlier test would not be supplied because the institution only has a 200 response.

We must first create a nock.js auxiliary file. This does three things in the following example:

- Specifying where we want to keep our fixtures.

- Setting the mode to record so that when tests are performed, we both record and utilize fixtures, as opposed to the normal dry run, which just uses existing institutions but does not record new ones.

- Using the afterRecord option, we can take various actions on our fixtures to improve their readability.

This may then be accessed in test files through const defaultOptions = require('./helpers/nock');/import defaultOptions from './helpers/nock';.

"Nock.back" may be used with either Promises or Async/Await; examples of both are provided. We'll discuss at the latter in this section.

```
it('should return a user', async () => { nock.back.
setMode('record'); const { nockDone } = await nock.
back(
    'user-data.json',
    defaultOptions,
  ); const userInfo = await query.getRandomUser();
expect(userInfo).toEqual(
    expect.objectContaining({
      results: expect.any(Object),
    }),
  ); nockDone();
nock.back.setMode('wild');});
```

We first mark the test as async so that we may utilize await. We switched to recording mode. We pass it the name of the file to save our fixtures in, as well as the defaultOptions provided in our nock.js helper to make them more human-readable. On completion, we are provided with the nockDone function, which will be called after our expectations have been met.

We can now compare the outcome of getRandomUser() to our expectations. For the sake of simplicity, we will just claim that it will include results, which will contain an Object.

Following that, we set the mode to wild, as we do not want other tests to utilize the fixture in this scenario.

The fixtures themselves are fascinating to look at and may be found in the directory supplied in the nock.js helper.

Nock is a highly effective tool for increasing the dependability of tests that use external services and allows for higher test coverage by reevaluating tests that were previously deemed too flaky to implement.

As with any mock, it is the developer's job to ensure that the mocking does not go too far and that the test may still fail due to a change in functionality, or else it is useless.

Mocking Actions

Let's have a peek at some code.

This is the component we want to put to the test. It refers to Vuex activities.

```
<template>
  <div class="text-align-center">
    <input type="text" @input="actionInputIfTrue" />
    <button @click="actionClick()">Click</button>
  </div>
</template>

<script>
  import { mapActions } from 'vuex'

  export default {
    methods: {
      ...mapActions(['actionClick']),
      actionInputIfTrue: function
actionInputIfTrue(event) {
        const inputValue = event.target.value
        if (inputValue === 'input') {
          this.$store.dispatch('actionInput', {
inputValue })
        }
      }
    }
  }
</script>
```

We don't care what the actions perform or how the shop appears for the purposes of this test. All we need to understand is that these activities are being carried out at the right time and with the right value.

When we shallowMount our component, we must supply a dummy store to Vue in order to test this.

We may send the store to a – localVue instead of the standard Vue constructor. A localVue is a Vue constructor that may be modified without impacting the global Vue constructor.

Let's have a look at this:

```
import { shallowMount, createLocalVue } from '@vue/
test-utils'
import Vuex from 'vuex'
import Actions from '../../../src/components/
Actions'

const localVue = createLocalVue()
```

```
localVue.use(Vuex)

describe('Actions.vue', () => {
  let actions
  let store

  beforeEach(() => {
    actions = {
      actionClick: jest.fn(),
      actionInput: jest.fn()
    }
    store = new Vuex.Store({
      actions
    })
  })

  it('dispatches "actionInput" when input event value
is "input"', () => {
    const wrapper = shallowMount(Actions, { store,
localVue })
    const input = wrapper.find('input')
    input.element.value = 'input'
    input.trigger('input')
    expect(actions.actionInput).toHaveBeenCalled()
  })

  it('does not dispatch "actionInput" when the event
value is not "input"', () => {
    const wrapper = shallowMount(Actions, { store,
localVue })
    const input = wrapper.find('input')
    input.element.value = 'not input'
    input.trigger('input')
    expect(actions.actionInput).not.toHaveBeenCalled()
  })

  it('calls store action "actionClick" when button is
clicked', () => {
    const wrapper = shallowMount(Actions, { store,
localVue })
    wrapper.find('button').trigger('click')
    expect(actions.actionClick).toHaveBeenCalled()
  })
})
```

What's going on here? With the localVue.use method, we first instruct Vue to utilize Vuex. This is simply a wrapper for Vue.use.

Then, we create a fake store by invoking new Vuex.Store with our mock data. We just pass it actions since that's all we're interested in.

The activities are only fictitious functions. These mock functions provide techniques for determining whether or not the actions were called.

We can then assert in our tests that the action stub was called when it was supposed to be invoked.

Now, the manner we define the shop may be unfamiliar to you.

We're using beforeEach to guarantee that the store is clean before each test. beforeEach is a mocha hook that is executed before each test. In our test, we are reassigning the value of the store variables. The mock functions would have to be reset automatically if we didn't do this. It also allows us to alter the status of our tests without impacting subsequent tests.

The most significant aspect of this test is that we construct a fake Vuex store and then send it to Vue Test Utils.

So, now that we can mock actions, let's have a look at mocking getters.

Mocking Getters

```
<template>
  <div>
    <p v-if="inputValue">{{inputValue}}</p>
    <p v-if="clicks">{{clicks}}</p>
  </div>
</template>

<script>
  import { mapGetters } from 'vuex'

  export default {
    computed: mapGetters(['clicks', 'inputValue'])
  }
</script>
```

This is a rather straightforward component. It displays the outcome of the getters' clicks and inputValue. Again, we don't really care what those getters return; all that matters is that their output is appropriately presented.

Let's put it to the test:

```
import { shallowMount, createLocalVue } from '@vue/
test-utils'
import Vuex from 'vuex'
import Getters from '../../../src/components/Getters'

const localVue = createLocalVue()

localVue.use(Vuex)

describe('Getters.vue', () => {
  let getters
  let store

  beforeEach(() => {
    getters = {
      clicks: () => 2,
      inputValue: () => 'input'
    }

    store = new Vuex.Store({
      getters
    })
  })

  it('Renders "store.getters.inputValue" in first p
tag', () => {
    const wrapper = shallowMount(Getters, { store,
localVue })
    const p = wrapper.find('p')
    expect(p.text()).toBe(getters.inputValue())
  })

  it('Renders "store.getters.clicks" in second p tag',
() => {
    const wrapper = shallowMount(Getters, { store,
localVue })
    const p = wrapper.findAll('p').at(1)
    expect(p.text()).toBe(getters.clicks().toString())
  })
})
```

This is a comparable test to our activities test. We build a fake store before each test, pass it as an option when using shallowMount, and check that the value returned by our mock getters is displayed.

This is fantastic, but what if we want to ensure that our getters are returning the proper section of our state?

Mocking with Modules

Modules are helpful in collapsing our shop into smaller bits. They also ship getters. These will be useful in our experiments.

Let's take a closer look:

```
<template>
  <div>
    <button @click="moduleActionClick()">Click</button>
    <p>{{moduleClicks}}</p>
  </div>
</template>

<script>
  import { mapActions, mapGetters } from 'vuex'

  export default {
    methods: {
      ...mapActions(['moduleActionClick'])
    },

    computed: mapGetters(['moduleClicks'])
  }
</script>
```

Simple component with one action and one getter.

And now for the test:

```
import { shallowMount, createLocalVue } from '@vue/
test-utils'
import Vuex from 'vuex'
import MyComponent from '../../../src/components/
MyComponent'
import myModule from '../../../src/store/myModule'

const localVue = createLocalVue()
```

```
localVue.use(Vuex)

describe('MyComponent.vue', () => {
  let actions
  let state
  let store

  beforeEach(() => {
    state = {
      clicks: 2
    }

    actions = {
      moduleActionClick: jest.fn()
    }

    store = new Vuex.Store({
      modules: {
        myModule: {
          state,
          actions,
          getters: myModule.getters,
          namespaced: true
        }
      }
    })
  })

  it('calls store action "moduleActionClick" when
button is clicked', () => {
    const wrapper = shallowMount(MyComponent, { store,
localVue })
    const button = wrapper.find('button')
    button.trigger('click')
    expect(actions.moduleActionClick).
toHaveBeenCalled()
  })

  it('renders "state.clicks" in first p tag', () => {
    const wrapper = shallowMount(MyComponent, { store,
localVue })
    const p = wrapper.find('p')
```

```
      expect(p.text()).toBe(state.clicks.toString())
  })
})
```

Testing a Vuex Store

There are two methods for testing a Vuex store. The first technique is to independently unit test the getters, mutations, and actions. The second way is to build a storage and then test against it. We'll take a look at both options.

We'll make a basic counter shop to demonstrate how to test a Vuex store. There will be an increment mutation and an evenOrOdd getter in the store.

```
// mutations.js
export default {
  increment(state) {
    state.count++
  }
}
// getters.js
export default {
  evenOrOdd: state => (state.count % 2 === 0?  'even'
: 'odd')
```

Testing Getters, Mutations, and Actions Separately

Because getters, mutations, and actions are all JavaScript functions, they may be tested without the need of Vue Test Utils and Vuex.

The advantage of testing getters, mutations, and actions independently is that your unit tests are more comprehensive. When they fail, you immediately know what is wrong with your code. The disadvantage is that you will have to simulate Vuex methods such as commit and dispatch. This can result in a situation in which your unit tests pass but your production code fails due to erroneous mocks.

We'll build two test files, mutations.spec.js and getters.spec.js, as follows:

First, let's put the increment mutations to the test:

```
// mutations.spec.js

import mutations from './mutations'
```

```
test('"increment" increments "state.count" by 1', ()
=> {
  const state = {
    count: 0
  }
  mutations.increment(state)
  expect(state.count).toBe(1)
})
```

Let's put the evenOrOdd getter to the test now. We can test it by constructing a mock state, passing it to the getter, and ensuring that it returns the proper result.

```
// getters.spec.js

import getters from './getters'

test('"evenOrOdd" returns even if "state.count" is
even', () => {
  const state = {
    count: 2
  }

  expect(getters.evenOrOdd(state)).toBe('even')
})
test('"evenOrOdd" returns odd if "state.count" is
odd', () => {
  const state = {
    count: 1
  }
  expect(getters.evenOrOdd(state)).toBe('odd')
})
```

Testing a Running Store
Another method for testing a Vuex store is to use the store config to establish a running store.

We don't have to simulate any Vuex functionalities by constructing a running store instance.

When a test fails, it might be difficult to pinpoint the source of the problem.

Let's make a test. To avoid cluttering the Vue basic constructor, we'll use localVue when creating a store. Using the store-config.js export, the test establishes a store:

```js
// store-config.js

import mutations from './mutations'
import getters from './getters'

export default {
  state: {
    count: 0
  },
  mutations,
  getters
}
// store-config.spec.js

import { createLocalVue } from '@vue/test-utils'
import Vuex from 'vuex'
import storeConfig from './store-config'
import { cloneDeep } from 'lodash'

test('increments "count" value when "increment" is
committed', () => {
  const localVue = createLocalVue()
  localVue.use(Vuex)
  const store = new Vuex.Store(cloneDeep(storeConfig))
  expect(store.state.count).toBe(0)
  store.commit('increment')
  expect(store.state.count).toBe(1)
})

test('updates "evenOrOdd" getter when "increment" is
committed', () => {
  const localVue = createLocalVue()
  localVue.use(Vuex)
  const store = new Vuex.Store(cloneDeep(storeConfig))
  expect(store.getters.evenOrOdd).toBe('even')
  store.commit('increment')
  expect(store.getters.evenOrOdd).toBe('odd')
})
```

We use cloneDeep to clone the store configuration before building a store with it. This is due to Vuex modifying the options object used to construct the store. To ensure that each test has a clean store, we must clone the storeConfig object.

CloneDeep, on the other hand, is not "deep" enough to clone storage modules. If your storeConfig contains modules, you must supply an object to new Vuex.Store(), as shown below:

```
import myModule from './myModule'
// ...
const store = new Vuex.Store({ modules: { myModule:
cloneDeep(myModule) } })
```

VUE.JS-TESTING-LIBRARY

When it comes to developing dependable apps, tests may play a vital part in an individual's or team's capacity to create new features, modify code, resolve errors, and so on. While there are several schools of thought on testing.

Unit Testing

Introduction
Individual units of code may be tested independently using unit tests. Unit testing is intended to give developers confidence in their code. You obtain assurance that your application will remain functional and stable when new features are introduced or code is refactored by creating detailed, effective tests.

Unit testing a Vue application is not dissimilar to testing other types of apps.

Choosing Your Framework
Because unit testing advice is frequently framework-independent, here are some general principles to bear in mind when deciding which unit testing tool is ideal for your application.

Excellent Mistake Reporting
It is vital that your unit testing framework offers helpful errors when tests fail. The assertion library is in charge of this. An assertion with high-quality error messages reduces the time required to debug the problem. In addition to just reporting which tests are failing, assertion libraries give information for why a test fails, such as what was expected against what was obtained.

Assertion libraries are included in several unit testing frameworks, such as Jest. Others, like as Mocha, need the installation of assertion libraries individually (usually Chai).

- Community and team participation are encouraged.

  Because the majority of unit testing frameworks are open-source, having an active community might be crucial for some teams who will be maintaining their tests for a long time and need to assure that a project will be continuously maintained. Furthermore, having an active community provides additional help should you run into problems.

  Vue Testing Library extends DOM Testing Library by providing APIs for interacting with Vue components. It is based on @vue/test-utils, Vue's official testing library.

- Vue Testing Library on GitHub

  Vue Testing Library, in a nutshell, does three things:

  1. DOM Testing Library query tools and helpers are re-exports.

  2. @vue/test-utils functions that are incompatible with Testing Library are hidden.

  3. Some methods from both sources are tweaks.

Installation

This module is supplied via npm and should be installed as a devDependency in your project:

```
npm install --save-dev @testing-library/vue
```

This library includes peerDependencies for Vue and vue-template-compiler.

You might also want to install @testing-library/jest-dom to utilize the custom Jest matchers.

Example:

```
<template>
  <div>
    <p>Times clicked: {{ count }}</p>
    <button @click="increment">increment</button>
  </div>
</template>
```

```
<script>
  export default {
    name: 'Button',
    data: () => ({
      count: 0,
    }),
    methods: {
      increment() {
        this.count++
      },
    },
  }
</script>
import {render, screen, fireEvent} from '@testing-
library/vue'
import Button from './Button'

test('increments value on click', async () => {
  // The 'render' method renders component into
the document.
  // It also binds to 'screen' all available
queries with which to interact
  // the component.
  render(Button)

  // queryByText returns first matching node for
the provided text
  // or returns null.
  expect(screen.queryByText('Times clicked: 0')).
toBeTruthy()

  // getByText retrieves the first node that
matches the specified text
  // or throws an error.
  const button = screen.getByText('increment')

  // Click a couple of times.
  await fireEvent.click(button)
  await fireEvent.click(button)

  expect(screen.queryByText('Times clicked: 2')).
toBeTruthy()
})
```

What Is Vue Testing Library?

Vue Testing Library is a lightweight Vue testing library that adds lightweight utility methods to @vue/test-utils. It was designed with a single guiding idea in mind: the more your tests mimic how your program is used, the more confidence they can provide you.

Why Use Vue Testing Library?

- You want to develop tests that aren't concerned with implementation details, such as checking how the solution is implemented rather than whether it provides the intended result.

- You want to develop tests that focus on the DOM nodes rather than the displayed Vue components.

- You want to develop tests that query the DOM like a user would.

How Vue Testing Library Works

Vue Testing Library works by providing utilities for querying the DOM in the same manner that a user would. These tools allow you to search for objects based on their label text, identify links and buttons based on their text content, and ensure that your Vue application is completely accessible.

In circumstances when it does not make sense or is impractical to discover items by their text content or label, Vue testing Library recommends utilizing data-tested attribute as an escape hatch for locating these components.

The data-tested property is applied to the HTML element that you intend to query in your test.

Example:

```
<button data-testid="checkoutButton">Check Out
</button>
```

Getting Started with Vue Testing Library

Now that you understand why you should use Vue Testing Library and how it works, let's get started by installing it in a fresh Vue CLI-generated Vue project.

To begin, execute the following command into the terminal (assuming you have Vue CLI installed on your system) to build a new Vue application:

```
vue create vue-testing-library-demo
```

Jest, a test runner built by Facebook, will be used to execute our tests. Jest may be simply installed using the Vue CLI plugin. Let's include that plugin:

```
vue add unit-jest
```

You will notice plugin added a new script in package.json:

```
"test:unit": "vue-cli-service test:unit",
```

This is where the tests would be conducted. It also created a new tests folder in src, as well as a unit folder with an example test file named example. spec.js. When we do npm run test:unit, it is based on the setup of Jest. Jest will search the tests directory for files and execute them. Let's run the following sample test file:

```
npm run test:unit
```

This should cause the example to execute. The spec.js test file is located in the tests/unit directory. Let's have a look at what's in this file:

```
import { shallowMount } from '@vue/test-utils'
import HelloWorld from '@/components/HelloWorld.vue'
describe('HelloWorld.vue', () => {
  it('renders props.msg when passed', () => {
    const msg = 'new message'
    const wrapper = shallowMount(HelloWorld, {
      propsData: { msg }
    })
    expect(wrapper.text()).toMatch(msg)
  })
})
```

Installing Jest with the Vue CLI plugin will automatically install @vue/test-utils, thus the preceding test file makes use of the shallowMount method from @vue/test-utils. To become acquainted with Vue Testing Library, just alter this identical test file to utilize Vue Testing Library rather than @vue/test-utils.

We'd start by removing @vue/test-utils because we won't be using it.

```
npm uninstall @vue/test-utils --save-dev
```

The Vue Testing Library is then installed as a development dependency:

```
npm install @testing-library/vue --save-dev
```

Then we proceed to make changes tests/unit/example.spec.js to this:

```
import { render } from '@testing-library/vue'
import HelloWorld from '@/components/HelloWorld.vue'
describe('HelloWorld.vue', () => {
  it('renders props.msg when passed', () => {
    const msg = 'new message'
    const { getByText } = render(HelloWorld, {
      props: { msg }
    })
    getByText(msg)
  })
})
```

If you run the test again, it should still pass. Let's have a look at what we did:

- To render the HelloWorld components, we utilize the render method given by Vue Testing Library. In the Vue Testing Library, the only way to render components is via render. You pass the Vue component and an optional options object when you call render.

- The options object is then used to provide in the message props required by the HelloWorld component. render will return an object containing utility methods for querying the DOM, one of which is getByText.

- Then, we use getByText to check the DOM for an element containing the text "new message."

You may have noticed a shift in emphasis from testing the visible Vue component to what the user sees in the DOM at this time. This change will allow you to test your apps from the user's point of view rather than focused on implementation specifics.

Quickstart

```
npm install --save-dev @testing-library/vue
```

All of the DOM Testing Library's getBy, getAllBy, queryBy, and query-AllBy commands are now available. The whole list of inquiries can be seen here.

You might also want to install @testing-library/jest-dom to utilize the specialized Jest matchers for the DOM.

The Problem

You want to develop test cases that are easy to maintain for your Vue components. You want your tests to avoid adding implementation details of your components as part of this aim. You'd rather concentrate on ensuring that your tests provide you with the confidence you need.

The Solution

Vue Testing Library is a lightweight testing solution for Vue components. It adds light utility methods on top of @vue/test-utils, encouraging improved testing habits.

Its main guiding idea is that the more your tests mimic how your product is used, the more trust you may have in them.

As a result, instead of dealing with instances of displayed Vue components, your tests will deal with actual DOM nodes.

The utilities provided by this package make it possible to query the DOM in the same way that a user would. They allow you to discover objects by their label text, as well as links and buttons, and they state that your application is accessible.

It also offers a data-tested suggested technique to identify items as an "escape hatch" for elements when the text content and label do not make sense or are impractical.

A basic example:

```
<template>
  <div>
    <p>Times clicked: {{ count }}</p>
    <button @click="increment">increment</button>
  </div>
</template>
```

```
<script>
  export default {
    name: 'Button',
    data: () => ({
      count: 0,
    }),
    methods: {
      increment() {
        this.count++
      },
    },
  }
</script>
```

```
import {render, screen, fireEvent} from '@testing-
library/vue'
import Button from './Button'

test('increments value on click', async () => {
  // 'render' method renders the component into
the document.
  // It also binds to 'screen' all available
queries to interact with the component. ("@
testing-library/vue - Documentation, Popularity |
Stackleap")
  render(Button)

  // queryByText retrieves the first node that
matches the specified text
  // or returns null.
  expect(screen.queryByText('Times clicked: 0')).
toBeTruthy()

  // getByText retrieves the first node that
matches the specified text
  // or throws an error.
  const button = screen.getByText('increment')

  // Click a couple of times.
  await fireEvent.click(button)
  await fireEvent.click(button)

  expect(screen.queryByText('Times clicked: 2')).
toBeTruthy()
})
```

Install @testing-library/jest-dom to provide useful assertions like.toBeIn-TheDocument (). You may write expect(screen.queryByText('Times clicked: 0')).toBeInTheDocument in the above example ().

Using byText queries isn't the only or best technique to find components. To learn about other options, see which query should I use? In the above example, getByRole('button', {name: 'increment'}) is perhaps the best approach for obtaining the button element.

CONCLUSION

We learned about NOCK and Vue.js-testing-library in this chapter, including what they are and how they are utilized. Forms and form validation will be discussed in the next chapter.

CHAPTER 9

Forms and Validation

IN THIS CHAPTER

➤ Form basics

➤ JavaScript forms validation

We learned about NOCK and Vue in Chapter 8. We also learned what JS-testing-libraries are and how they work. We will learn about forms and form validation in this chapter.

FORM BASICS

To create form in HTML, you use the <form> element: ("JavaScript Form Archives - Tutorial")

```
<form action="/signup" method="post" id="signup">
</form>
```

- The action is a URL that is used to process the form submission. The action in this case is the/signup URL.

- The method specifies which HTTP method should be used to submit the form. Either post or get is the way.

When you want to obtain data from the server, you usually use the get method, and when you want to alter something on the server, you usually use the post method.

DOI: 10.1201/9781003310464-9

The HTMLFormElement object in JavaScript is used to represent a form. The HTMLFormElement has the properties listed below, which correspond to HTML attributes:

- **action:** It is the URL where the form data is processed. It is comparable to the <form> element's action property.

- **method:** It is the HTTP method that corresponds to the <form> element's method property.

In addition, the HTMLFormElement element has the following handy methods:

- **submit():** submit the form.

- **reset():** reset the form.

Referencing Forms

You can use getElementById() or const form = document. getElementById('subscribe') to refer to the form element in the DOM: const form = document.getElementById('subscribe');

JavaScript is the coding language (javascript)

There can be several forms in an HTML document. The document.forms property returns a list of forms on the document (HTMLFormControlsCollection):

```
document.forms
```

An index is used to find a specific form. The following statement, for example, returns the HTML document in its initial form:

```
document.forms[0]
CSS (css)
```

Submitting a Form

A submit button is usually present on a form. The browser delivers form data to the server when you click it. To make a submit button, use the type submit in the <input> or <button> element:

```
<input type="submit" value="Subscribe">
Code language: HTML, XML (xml)
```

Or

```
<button type="submit">Subscribe</button>
```
Code language: HTML, XML (xml)

When you press the Enter key while the submit button is highlighted, the browser submits the form input as well.

When you submit the form, submit event is called before the request is sent to the server. This allows you to check the form data for accuracy. You can stop submitting the form if the data is invalid.

Use the form element's addEventListener() function to add an event listener to the submit event as follows:

```
const form  = document.getElementById('signup');

form.addEventListener('submit', (event) => {
    // handle the form data
});
```
Code language: JavaScript (javascript)

To prevent the form from being submitted, execute the event object's preventDefault() function from within the submit event handler, as illustrated below:

```
form.addEventListener('submit', (event) => {
    // stop form submission
    event.preventDefault();
});
```
Code language: PHP (php)

If the form data is invalid, you usually invoke the event.preventDefault() method.

The submit() method of the form object is used to submit the form in JavaScript:

```
form.submit();
```
Code language: CSS (css)

The form.submit() function does not fire the submit event. As a result, before using this approach, you should carefully validate the form.

Accessing Form Fields

You can utilize DOM techniques like getElementsByName(), getElement-ById(), querySelector(), and others to retrieve form fields.

You may also use the form object's elements property. A collection of form elements is stored in the form.elements property.

You can access an element in JavaScript by index, id, or name. Consider the following signup form, which has two input> elements:

```html
<form action="signup.html" method="post" id="signup">
      <h1>Sign Up</h1>
      <div class="field">
              <label for="name">Name:</label>
              <input type="text" id="name" name="name"
placeholder="Enter fullname" />
              <small></small>
      </div>
      <div class="field">
              <label for="email">Email:</label>
              <input type="text" id="email"
name="email" placeholder="Enter email address" />
              <small></small>
      </div>
      <button type="submit">Subscribe</button>
</form>
Code language: HTML, XML (xml)
```

To get to the form's elements, you must first get the form element:

```javascript
const form = document.getElementById('signup');
Code language: JavaScript (javascript)
To access the element, use index, id, or name. The
first form element is accessed as follows:

form.elements[0]; // by index
form.elements['name']; // by name
form.elements['name']; // by id (name & id are the
same in this case)
Code language: JavaScript (javascript)
```

The following accesses the second input element:

```javascript
form.elements[1]; // by index
form.elements['email']; // by name
form.elements['email']; // by id
Code language: JavaScript (javascript)
```

After accessing form field, you can use value property to access its value, for example:

```javascript
const form = document.getElementById('signup');
const name = form.elements['name'];
const email = form.elements['email'];

// getting element's value
let fullName = name.value;
let emailAddress = email.value;
```

Put It All Together: Signup Form

The following is an example of an HTML document including a signup form.

```html
<!DOCTYPE html>
<html lang="en">
        <head>
                <title>JavaScript Form Demo</title>
                <meta name="viewport" content="width=device-
width, initial-scale=2.0" />
                <link rel="stylesheet" href="css/style.css" />
        </head>
        <body>
                <div class="container">
                        <form action="signup.html" method="post"
id="signup">
                                <h1>Sign Up</h1>
                                <div class="field">
                                        <label
for="name">Name:</label>
                                                <input type="text"
id="name" name="name" placeholder="Enter fullname" />
                                        <small></small>
                                </div>
                                <div class="field">
                                        <label for="email">
Email:</label>
```

```html
                              <input type="text"
id="email" name="email" placeholder="Enter email address" />
                              <small></small>
                    </div>
                    <div class="field">
                            <button type="submit"
class="full">Subscribe</button>
                        </div>
                    </form>
              </div>
              <script src="js/app.js"></script>
        </body>
</html>
```

Code language: HTML, XML (xml)

The style.css and app.js files are referenced in the HTML text. The <small> element is used to display an error message if the data in the <input> element is invalid.

The following error will occur if you submit the form without providing any information: The following error will occur if you submit the form with your name but an invalid email address format:

The whole app.js file is shown below:

```javascript
// show message with a type of the input
function showMessage(input, message, type) {
        // get tsmall element and set the message
        const msg = input.parentNode.
querySelector("small");
        msg.innerText = message;
        // update the class for the input
        input.className = type? "success" : "error";
        return type;
}

function showError(input, message) {
        return showMessage(input, message, false);
}

function showSuccess(input) {
        return showMessage(input, "", true);
}
```

```javascript
function hasValue(input, message) {
        if (input.value.trim() === "") {
                return showError(input, message);
        }
        return showSuccess(input);
}

function validateEmail(input, requiredMsg, invalidMsg) {
        // check if the value is not empty
        if (!hasValue(input, requiredMsg)) {
                return false;
        }
        // validate email format
        const emailRegex =
                /^(([^<>()\[\]\\.,;:\s@"]+(\.[^<>()\
[\]\\.,;:\s@"]+)*)|(".+"))@((\[[0-9]{1,3}\.[0-9]{1,3}\.
[0-9]{1,3}\.[0-9]{1,3}\])|(([a-zA-Z\-0-9]+\.)+[a-zA-Z]
{2,}))$/;

        const email = input.value.trim();
        if (!emailRegex.test(email)) {
                return showError(input, invalidMsg);
        }
        return true;
}

const form = document.querySelector("#signup");

const NAME_REQUIRED = "Enter your name";
const EMAIL_REQUIRED = "Enter your email";
const EMAIL_INVALID = "Enter correct email address format";

form.addEventListener("submit", function (event) {
        // stop form-submission
        event.preventDefault();

        // validate form
        let nameValid = hasValue(form.elements["name"],
NAME_REQUIRED);
        let emailValid = validateEmail(form.
elements["email"], EMAIL_REQUIRED, EMAIL_INVALID);
        // if valid, submit form.
        if (nameValid && emailValid) {
                alert("Demo only. No form was
posted.");
        }
});
```

Code language: JavaScript

How It Works

The showMessage() Function

"The showMessage() function accepts an input element, message, and a type:" ("Get form name via JavaScript")

```javascript
// show message with a type of the input
function showMessage(input, message, type) {
        // get <small> element and set the message
        const msg = input.parentNode.querySelector("small");
        msg.innerText = message;
        // update class for the input
        input.className = type?  "success"  :  "error";
        return type;
}
```

Code language: JavaScript

The following shows name input field on the form:

```html
<div class="field">
        <label for="name">Name:</label>
        <input type="text" id="name" name="name"
placeholder="Enter fullname" />
        <small></small>
</div>
```

Code language: HTML, XML (xml)

If name's value is blank, you need to get its parent first which is <div> with class "field".

```css
input.parentNode
```

Code language: CSS (css)

Next, you need to select <small> element:

```javascript
const msg = input.parentNode.querySelector("small");
```

Code language: JavaScript

Then, we updatemessage:

```javascript
msg.innerText = message;
```

The CSS class of the input field is then changed based on the type parameter value. If the type is true, we set the input's class to success. Otherwise, the class is set to error.

```javascript
input.className = type?  "success" : "error";
```

Code language: JavaScript (javascript)

Finally, return the value of the type:

```javascript
return type;
```

Code language: JavaScript (javascript)

The functions showError() and showSuccess() are used to display errors and successes, respectively.

The showMessage() function is called by the showError() and showSuccess() routines. The function showError() always returns false, but the function showSuccess() always returns true. The error message is also set to an empty string by the showSuccess() method.

```javascript
function showError(input, message) {
        return showMessage(input, message, false);
}
```

```javascript
function showSuccess(input) {
        return showMessage(input, "", true);
}
```

Code language: JavaScript (javascript)

The hasValue() Function

The hasValue() function determines whether an input element has a value and displays an error message or a success message using the showError() or showSuccess() functions, as appropriate:

```javascript
function hasValue(input, message) {
    if (input.value.trim() === "") {
        return showError(input, message);
    }
    return showSuccess(input);
}
```

Code language: JavaScript (javascript)

The validateEmail() Function

The validateEmail() function validates if email field contains a valid email address:

```php
function validateEmail(input, requiredMsg, invalidMsg) {
    // check if value is not empty
    if (!hasValue(input, requiredMsg)) {
        return false;
    }
    // validate email format
    const emailRegex =
        /^((([^<>()\[\]\\.,;:\s@"]+(\.[^<>()\
[\]\\.,;:\s@"]+)*)|(".+"))@((\[[0-9]{1,3}\.[0-9]{1,3}\.
[0-9]{1,3}\.[0-9]{1,3}\])|(([a-zA-Z\-0-9]+\.)+[a-zA-Z]
{2,}))$/;

    const email = input.value.trim();
    if (!emailRegex.test(email)) {
        return showError(input, invalidMsg);
    }
    return true;
}
```

Code language: PHP (php)

The validateEmail() method calls the hasValue() function to see if the field value is empty. It displays the requiredMsg if the input field is empty.

To validate the email, a regular expression is employed. The invalid Msg variable is returned by the validateEmail() function if the email is invalid.

The Submit Event Handler

To begin, use the querySelector() method to choose the signup form by its id:

```javascript
const form = document.querySelector("#signup");
```

Code language: JavaScript

Second, create some variables for storing error messages:

```javascript
const NAME_REQUIRED = "Enter your name";
const EMAIL_REQUIRED = "Enter your email";
const EMAIL_INVALID = "Enter correct email address format";
```

Code language: JavaScript (javascript)

Third, add submit event listener of the signup form using the addEvent Listener() method:

```javascript
form.addEventListener("submit", function (event) {
        // stop form submission
        event.preventDefault();

        // validate form
        let nameValid = hasValue(form.elements["name"],
NAME_REQUIRED);
        let emailValid = validateEmail(form.
elements["email"], EMAIL_REQUIRED, EMAIL_INVALID);
        // if valid, submit form.
        if (nameValid && emailValid) {
                alert("Demo only. No form was posted.");
        }
});
```

Code language: JavaScript (javascript)

In the submit event handler:

1. Call the event to halt the submission of the form. preventDefault() is a method that prevents anything from happening by default.

2. Use the hasValue() and validateEmail() functions to validate the name and email fields.

3. Display an alert if both the name and the email address are correct. You must call the form in a real-world application. To submit the form, use the submit() method.

Summary

- To build an HTML form, use the form> element.

- To pick a form> element, use DOM techniques like getDocument-ById() and querySelector(). The form element is also returned via a number index in document.forms[index].

- To access form elements, use form.elements.

- The submit event is triggered when users click the form's submit button.

JAVASCRIPT FORM VALIDATION

JavaScript is capable of validating HTML forms.

If a form field (fname) is empty, this method sends a message and returns false, preventing the form from being uploaded:

```
JavaScript Example
function validateForm() {
  let x = document.forms["myForm"]["fname"].value;
  if (x == "") {
    alert("Name must filled out");
    return false;
  }
}
```

The function can call when the form is submitted:

```
HTML Form Example
<form name="myForm" action="/action_page.
php" onsubmit="return validateForm()" method="post">
Name: <input type="text" name="fname">
<input type="submit" value="Submit">
</form>
```

JavaScript Has the Ability to Validate Numerical Input

Numeric input is frequently validated using JavaScript:

Please enter a value between 1 and 10

┌─────────┐
│   │ Submit
└─────────┘

Automatic HTML Form Validation

Validation of HTML forms can be done automatically by the browser.

The needed attribute stops this form from being submitted if a form field (fname) is empty:

```
HTML Form Example
<form action="/action_page.php" method="post">
  <input type="text" name="fname" required>
  <input type="submit" value="Submit">
</form>
```

Internet Explorer 9 and earlier don't support automatic HTML form validation.

Data Validation

The process of ensuring that user information is clean, correct, and helpful is known as data validation.

Validation tasks include:

- Has the user completed all the essential fields?
- Is the date entered by the user correct?
- Did the user type text into a numerical field?

The most common goal of data validation is to ensure that user input is correct. Validation can be defined in a variety of ways and implemented in a variety of ways. After input has been transmitted to the server, a web server performs server side validation. A web browser performs client-side validation before sending data to a web server.

HTML Constraint Validation

Constraint validation is a new HTML validation technique introduced in HTML5.

Validation of HTML constraints is based on:

- Validate HTML Input Attributes with constraints.

- Validate CSS Pseudo Selectors with constraints.

- Validate DOM Properties and Methods with constraints.

Constraint-Validation HTML Input Attributes

Attribute	Description
Disabled	Specifies that input element should be disabled
Max	Specifies maximum value of an input element
Min	Specifies minimum value of an input element
Pattern	Specifies value pattern of an input element
Required	Specifies that input field requires an element
Type	Specifies type of an input element

Constraint-Validation CSS Pseudo Selectors

Selector	Description
:disabled	Selects input elements with "disabled" attribute specified
:invalid	Selects input elements with the invalid values
:optional	Selects the input elements with no "required" attribute specified
:required	Selects input elements with "required" attribute specified
:valid	Selects input elements with the valid values

Basic Usage

On form input, textarea, and select elements, the v-model directive can be used to build two-way data connections. It selects the appropriate technique for updating the element based on the input type. V-model is syntax sugar for updating data on user input events, with special attention paid to specific edge circumstances.

Any form element's initial value, checked, or chosen properties will be ignored by v-model. The Vue instance data will always be seen as the source of truth. The initial value should be declared on the JavaScript side, in the data option of your component.

For different input components, v-model uses different properties and emits distinct events:

- Value property and input event are used by text and textarea elements;

- Checked property and change event are used by checkboxes and radiobuttons;

- Select fields make use of value as a prop and change as an event.

You will observe that v-model is not updated during IME construction for languages that require an IME. If you want to cater to these changes as well, use the input event instead.

Text:

```
<input v-model="message" placeholder="edit me">
<p>Message is: {{ message }}</p>
```

edit me

Message is:

Message block.

Multiline text:

```
<span>Multiline message is:</span>
<p style="white-space: pre-line;">{{ message }}</p>
<br>
<textarea v-model="message" placeholder="add multiple
lines"></textarea>
```

Multiline message is:

add multiple lines

Multiline message block.

Checkbox:

Single checkbox, boolean value:

```
<input type="checkbox" id="checkbox"
v-model="checked">
<label for="checkbox">{{ checked }}</label>
```

☐ false

Block of checkbox.

Multiple checkboxes, bound to the same Array:

```
<input type="checkbox" id="jacky" value="Jack"
v-model="checkedNames">
<label for="jack">Jacky</label>
<input type="checkbox" id="johny" value="John"
v-model="checkedNames">
<label for="john">Johny</label>
<input type="checkbox" id="midny" value="Mike"
v-model="checkedNames">
<label for="mike">Midny</label>
<br>
<span>Checked names: {{ checkedNames }}</span>
new Vue({
  el: '...',
  data: {
    checkedNames: []
  }
})
```

☐ Jack ☐ John ☐ Mike
Checked names: []

Block of multi checkbox.

Radio:

```
<input type="radio" id="one" value="One"
v-model="picked">
<label for="one">One</label>
<br>
<input type="radio" id="two" value="Two"
v-model="picked">
<label for="two">Two</label>
<br>
<span>Picked: {{ picked }}</span>
```

○ One
○ Two
Picked:

Radio button example.

Select:

Single select:

```
<select v-model="selected">
  <option disabled value="">Please select one</option>
  <option>A</option>
  <option>B</option>
  <option>C</option>
</select>
<span>Selected: {{ selected }}</span>
new Vue({
  el: '...',
  data: {
    selected: ''
  }
})
```

Please select one ⌄ Selected:

Select button example.

Multiple select (bound to Array):

```
<select v-model="selected" multiple>
  <option>A</option>
  <option>B</option>
  <option>C</option>
</select>
<br>
<span>Selected: {{ selected }}</span>
```

A
B
C

Selected: []

Select list example.

Dynamic Options Rendered with v-for

```
<select v-model="selected">
  <option v-for="option in options"
v-bind:value="option.value">
```

```
    {{ option.text }}
  </option>
</select>
<span>Selected: {{ selected }}</span>
new Vue({
  el: '...',
  data: {
    selected: 'A',
    options: [
      { text: 'One', value: 'A' },
      { text: 'Two', value: 'B' },
      { text: 'Three', value: 'C' }
    ]
  }
})
```

Value Bindings

The v-model binding values for radio, checkbox, and select choices are normally static strings (or booleans for checkboxes):

```
<!-- 'picked' is a string "a" when check -->
<input type="radio" v-model="picked" value="a">

<!-- 'toggle' is true or false -->
<input type="checkbox" v-model="toggle">

"<!-- 'selected' is a string "abc" when first option
is selected -->" ("Essentials - Form Input Bindings
- 《Vue 3 Document (3.0.0 ...")
<select v-model="selected">
  <option value="abc">ABC</option>
</select>
```

There are situations when we want to associate the value with a Vue instance's dynamic property. To accomplish this, we can use v-bind. We may also use v-bind to tie the input value to non-string values.

Checkbox:

```
<input
  type="checkbox"
  v-model="toggle"
  true-value="yes"
  false-value="no"
```

```
>
// when checked:
vm.toggle === 'yes'
// when unchecked:
vm.toggle === 'no'
```

Radio:

```
<input type="radio" v-model="pick" v-bind:value="a">
// when checked:
vm.pick === vm.a
```

Select options:

```
<select v-model="selected">
  <!-- inline object literal -->
  <option v-bind:value="{ number: 123 }">123</option>
</select>
// when selected:
typeof vm.selected // => 'object'
vm.selected.number // => 123
```

Modifiers

.lazy

By default, v-model synchronizes the input with the data after each input event (except for IME composition, as stated above). Instead of syncing after change events, you can use the lazy modifier:

```
<!-- synced after "change" instead of "input" -->
<input v-model.lazy="msg">
```

.number

If you wish user input to be automatically typecast as a Number, you may add the number modifier to your v-model controlled inputs:

```
<input v-model.number="age" type="number">
```

This is useful because the value of HTML input elements is always a string, even when type="number." If parseFloat() fails to parse the value, the original value is returned.

.trim

You may use the trim modifier on your v-model-managed inputs to auto-matically trim whitespace from user input:

```
<input v-model.trim="msg">
```

v-model with Components

The built-in input types in HTML will not always suffice. Vue components, on the other hand, allow you to create reusable inputs with completely configurable behavior. These inputs are even compatible with the v-model!

The Basics

On form input elements, the v-model directive can be used to build two-way data bindings. It selects the appropriate technique for updating the element based on the input type.

Example:

```
1   <form id="demo">
2     <!-- text -->
3     <p>
4       <input type="text" v-model="msg">
5       {{msg}}
6     </p>
7     <!-- checkbox -->
8     <p>
9       <input type="checkbox" v-model="checked">
10      {{checked? "yes" : "no"}}
11    </p>
12    <!-- radio buttons -->
13    <p>
14      <input type="radio" name="picked"
          value="one" v-model="picked">
15      <input type="radio" name="picked"
          value="two" v-model="picked">
16      {{picked}}
17    </p>
18    <!-- select -->
19    <p>
```

```
20      <select v-model="selected">
21        <option>one</option>
22        <option>two</option>
23      </select>
24      {{selected}}
25    </p>
26    <!-- multiple select -->
27    <p>
28      <select v-model="multiSelect" multiple>
29        <option>one</option>
30        <option>two</option>
31        <option>three</option>
32      </select>
33      {{multiSelect}}
34    </p>
35    <p><pre>data: {{$data | json 2}}</pre></p>
36  </form>
 1  new Vue({
 2    el: '#demo',
 3    data: {
 4      msg        : 'hi!',
 5      checked    : true,
 6      picked     : 'one',
 7      selected   : 'two',
 8      multiSelect: ['one', 'three']
 9    }
10  })
```

Lazy Updates

After each input event, v-model synchronizes the input with the data by
default. You can change the behavior to sync after change events by adding
a lazy attribute:

```
1  <!-- synced after "change" instead of "input" -->
2  <input v-model="msg" lazy>
```

Casting Value as a Number

If you wish user input to be automatically stored as numbers, you may add
a number property to your v-model driven inputs:

```
1  <input v-model="age" number>
```

Bind to Expressions

^0.12.12 only

When utilizing the v-model on checkbox and radio inputs, the bound value is either a Boolean or a string:

```
1  <!-- toggle is either true or false -->
2  <input type="checkbox" v-model="toggle">
3
4  <!-- pick is "green" when this radio box is
     selected -->
5  <input type="radio" v-model="pick" value="green">
```

This can be a bit constraining; there are times when we would like to bind the underlying value to something else. Here is how to go about it:

Checkbox:

```
1  <input type="checkbox" v-model="toggle" true-
   exp="a" false-exp="b">
1  // when checked:
2  vm.toggle === vm.a
3  // when unchecked:
4  vm.toggle === vm.b
```

Radio:

```
1  <input type="radio" v-model="pick" exp="a">
1  // when checked:
2  vm.pick === vm.a
```

Dynamic Select Options

As you need to dynamically render a list of options for a choose> element, you should use an options attribute in conjunction with v-model so that v-model is properly synced when the options change:

```
1  <select v-model="selected" options="myOptions">
   </select>
```

MyOptions should be a keypath/expression in your data that links to an Array that will be used as its choices.

Plain strings can be found in the Array options:

```
1  options = ['a', 'b', 'c']
```

It can also contain items in the {text:", value:"} format. The option wording can be shown differently than the underlying value in this object format:

```
1  options = [
2    { text: 'A', value: 'a' },
3    { text: 'B', value: 'b' }
4  ]
```

Will render:

```
1  <select>
2    <option value="a">A</option>
3    <option value="b">B</option>
4  </select>
```

The value can also be Objects:
0.12.11+ only

```
1  options = [
2    { text: 'A', value: { msg: 'hello' }},
3    { text: 'B', value: { msg: 'bye' }}
4  ]
```

Option Groups
Alternatively, the object may be formatted as {label:", options:[...]}. It will be presented as an <optgroup> in this case:

```
1  [
2    { label: 'A', options: ['a', 'b']},
3    { label: 'B', options: ['c', 'd']}
4  ]
```

Will render:

```
1  <select>
2    <optgroup label="A">
3      <option value="a">a</option>
4      <option value="b">b</option>
5    </optgroup>
6    <optgroup label="B">
7      <option value="c">c</option>
```

```
 8       <option value="d">d</option>
 9     </optgroup>
10  </select>
```

Options Filter

It is possible that your source data will not be in this format, so you will have to change it to create dynamic choices. The options param supports filters to DRY up the transformation, and it can be useful to encapsulate your transformation logic inside a reusable custom filter:

```
1  Vue.filter('extract', function (value,
   keyToExtract) {
2    return value.map(function (item) {
3      return item[keyToExtract]
4    })
5  })
1  <select
2    v-model="selectedUser"
3    options="users | extract 'name'">
4  </select>
```

"The above filter transforms data like [{ name: 'Bruce' }, { name: 'Chuck' }] into ['Bruce', 'Chuck'] so it becomes properly formatted." ("Handling Forms - vue.js")

Static Default Option

0.12.10+ only

In addition to the dynamically produced choices, you can supply one static default option:

```
1  <select v-model="selectedUser" options="users">
2    <option value="">Select a user...</option>
3  </select>
```

After the static option, dynamic options created by users will be added. If the v-model value is false, the static option will be picked by default (excluding 0).

Input Debounce

The debounce parameter allows you to specify a minimum delay before the input data is synced to the model following each keystroke. When executing expensive activities on each update, such as making an Ajax request for type-ahead autocompletion, this can be handy.

```
1  <input v-model="msg" debounce="500">
```

Setting Up Our Vue.js App

We will begin by building a basic Vue.js app with some HTML markup. Bulma will also be imported so that we can take benefit of some ready-made styles:

```
<!DOCTYPE html>
<html>
<head>
  <title>Fun with Forms in Vue.js</title>
  <link rel="stylesheet" href="https://cdnjs.
cloudflare.com/ajax/libs/bulma/0.4.4/css/bulma.min.
css">
</head>

<body>
  <div class="columns" id="app">
    <div class="column is-two-thirds">
      <section class="section">
        <h1 class="title">Fun with Forms in Vue 2.0</h1>
        <p class="subtitle">
          Learn how to work with forms, including
<strong>validation</strong>!
        </p>
        <hr>

        <!-- form starts here -->
        <section class="form">

</section>
      </section>
    </div>
  </div>

<script src="https://cdnjs.cloudflare.com/ajax/libs/
vue/2.3.4/vue.min.js"></script>
```

```
<script>
  new Vue({
    el: '#app'
  })
</script>

</body>
</html>
```

Binding Input Values with v-model

Using the v-model directive, we can link form input and textarea element values to Vue instance data. The v-model directive, according to the Vue documentation, allows you to construct two-way data bindings on form input, textarea, and select components. It determines the appropriate way for updating the element based on the input type.

Text input example:

To begin, create a simple text entry to obtain a user's full name:

```
. . .
<section class="form">
  <div class="field">
    <label class="label">Name</label>
    <div class="control">
      <input v-model="form.name" class="input"
type="text" placeholder="Text input">
    </div>
  </div>
</section>
. . .

<script>
new Vue({
  el: '#app',
  data: {
    form : {
      name: ''
    }
  }
})
</script>
```

In the above code, we establish the data option in our Vue instance as well as a form object that will hold all the information we need for our form. Name is the first property we define, and it is bound to the text input we also generated.

We may utilize the value of form.name anywhere in our program now that two-way binding is available, as it will be the updated value of the text input. To see all the properties of our form object, we may add a section:

```
...
<div class="columns" id="app">
  <!-- // ... -->

<div class="column">
    <section class="section" id="results">
      <div class="box">
        <ul>
          <!-- Show the values of all the 'form'
attributes in a loop -->
          <li v-for="(item, k) in form">
            <strong>{{ k }}:</strong> {{ item }}
          </li>
        </ul>
      </div>
    </section>
  </div>
</div>
...
```

The value, checked, or chosen properties of form inputs are disregarded by v-model, which treats Vue instance data as the source of truth. This means that in the Vue instance, you can set a default value for form.name. That is what the form input's first value will be.

Textarea example:

These work the same way as regular input boxes work:

```
...
<div class="field">
  <label class="label">Message</label>
  <div class="control">
    <textarea class="textarea" placeholder="Message"
v-model="form.message"></textarea>
  </div>
</div>
...
```

And the corresponding value in the form model:

```
data: {
  form : {
    name: '',
    message: '' // textarea value
  }
}
```

It is vital to remember that two-way binding will not work with interpolation in textarea – textarea> form.message/textarea>. Instead, use the v-model directive.

Selecting boxes with the v-model directive

For select boxes, the v-model directive can also be readily plugged in. The value of the specified option will be synchronized with the defined model:

```
. . .
<div class="field">
  <label class="label">Inquiry Type</label>
  <div class="control">
    <div class="select">
      <select v-model="form.inquiry_type">
        <option disabled value="">Nothing selected</
option>
        <option v-for="option in options.inquiry"
v-bind:value="option.value">
          {{ option.text }}
        </option>
      </select>
    </div>
  </div>
</div>
. . .
```

We used the v-for directive in the above code to dynamically load the options. This necessitates defining the Vue instance's accessible options as well:

```
data: {
  form : {
    name: '',
```

```
      message: '',
      inquiry_type: '' // single select box value
    },
    options: {
      inquiry: [
        { value: 'feature', text: "Feature Request"},
        { value: 'bug', text: "Bug Report"},
        { value: 'support', text: "Support"}
      ]
    }
  }
}
```

A multi-select box follows the same procedure. The selected values for the multi-select box, on the other hand, are saved in an array.

Example:

```
...
<div class="field">
  <label class="label">LogRocket Usecases</label>
  <div class="control">
    <div class="select is-multiple">
      <select multiple v-model="form.
logrocket_usecases">
        <option>Debugging</option>
        <option>Fixing Errors</option>
        <option>User support</option>
      </select>
    </div>
  </div>
</div>
...
```

CONCLUSION

We learned about Vue.js forms and forms validation in this chapter, including what they are and how to utilize them.

Bibliography

#learning, A. A., & Agile. (2021, February 15). *Build a full-stack React app with zero configuration - Agile Actors #learning.* Agile Actors #learning; learningactors.com. https://learningactors.com/build-a-full-stack-react-app-with-zero-configuration/

@nirnejak. (n.d.). *7 advantages of using Vue.JS | The Progressive Framework.* 7 Advantages of Using Vue.JS | The Progressive Framework; www.inkoop.io. Retrieved July 11, 2022, from https://www.inkoop.io/blog/7-advantages-of-using-vue-js/

27. Setup (Reusability & Composition) - Vue.js 3 - W3cubDocs. (n.d.). 27. Setup (Reusability & Composition) - Vue.Js 3 - W3cubDocs; docs.w3cub.com. Retrieved July 11, 2022, from https://docs.w3cub.com/vue~3/guide/composition-api-setup.html

Adebayo-Oyetoro, A. (2019, November 14). *Using JSX with Vue - LogRocket Blog.* LogRocket Blog; blog.logrocket.com. https://blog.logrocket.com/using-jsx-with-vue/

admin. (2022, January 8). *JavaScript Form.* JavaScript Tutorial; www.javascripttutorial.net. https://www.javascripttutorial.net/javascript-dom/javascript-form/

Amaechi, A. (2021, February 4). *Styling a Vue.js application using CSS - LogRocket Blog.* LogRocket Blog; blog.logrocket.com. https://blog.logrocket.com/styling-a-vue-js-application-using-css/

Au-Yeung, J. (2020, April 19). *Programmatic Navigation of Vue Router Routes | by John Au-Yeung | JavaScript in Plain English.* Medium; javascript.plainenglish.io. https://javascript.plainenglish.io/programmatic-navigation-of-vue-router-routes-288b81cc5516

Au-Yeung, J. (2020, January 23). *Vue.js Basics: Inputs, Events, and Components | by John Au-Yeung | Better Programming.* Medium; betterprogramming.pub. https://betterprogramming.pub/vue-js-basics-inputs-events-and-components-1a874528e66a

Au-Yeung, J. (2021, February 6). *How to Get Query Parameters from a URL in Vue.js? - The Web Dev.* The Web Dev; thewebdev.info. https://thewebdev.info/2021/02/06/how-to-get-query-parameters-from-a-url-in-vue-js/

Bistolfi, N. (2021, July 5). *How to use images in Vue.js: A complete guide – Piio Blog.* How to Use Images in Vue.Js: A Complete Guide – Piio Blog; blog.piio.co. https://blog.piio.co/posts/how-to-use-images-in-vue-js

Chaudhari, M. (2021, August 16). *Optimizing Vue Apps: Lazy Loading and Code Splitting | by Mayank Chaudhari | Medium*. Medium; mayank-1513.medium. com. https://mayank-1513.medium.com/optimizing-vue-apps-lazy-loading-and-code-splitting-1036d27512fd

Dynamic Route Matching | Vue Router. (n.d.). Dynamic Route Matching | Vue Router; v3.router.vuejs.org. Retrieved July 11, 2022, from https://v3.router. vuejs.org/guide/essentials/dynamic-matching.html

Eluwande, Y. (2021, January 1). *A complete guide to forms in Vue.js - LogRocket Blog*. LogRocket Blog; blog.logrocket.com. https://blog.logrocket.com/an-imperative-guide-to-forms-in-vue-js-2/

Explaining the Vue Context Argument - A Composition API Tutorial. (n.d.). Explaining the Vue Context Argument - A Composition API Tutorial; learnvue.co. Retrieved July 11, 2022, from https://learnvue.co/2021/06/explaining-the-vue-context-argument-a-composition-api-tutorial/

Form Input Bindings — Vue.js. (n.d.). Form Input Bindings — Vue.Js; v2.vuejs. org. Retrieved July 11, 2022, from https://v2.vuejs.org/v2/guide/forms.html

Form Input Bindings | Vue.js. (n.d.). Form Input Bindings | Vue.Js; vuejs.org. Retrieved July 11, 2022, from https://vuejs.org/guide/essentials/forms.html

frankies. (n.d.). *Lazy Loading · vue-r-pdf*. Lazy Loading · Vue-r-Pdf; frankies1. gitbooks.io. Retrieved July 11, 2022, from https://frankies1.gitbooks.io/vue-r-pdf/content/en/advanced/lazy-loading.html

Fraser, D. (2018, July 17). *Mocking HTTP requests with Nock. This is a "how to" article on using... | by Dominic Fraser | codeburst*. Medium; codeburst.io. https://codeburst.io/testing-mocking-http-requests-with-nock-480e3f164851

Galyamov, R. (2019, July 21). *How to programmatically navigate using router in Vue.js – Renat Galyamov*. Renat Galyamov; renatello.com. https://renatello.com/vue-js-navigate-programmatically/

GARG, S. (2019, December 31). *Context API for Vue.js/Nuxt.js applications | by SHIV GARG | Technology at upGrad*. Medium; engineering. upgrad.com. https://engineering.upgrad.com/context-api-for-vue-js-nuxt-js-applications-e4c984508bd1

Get form name via JavaScript. (n.d.). Get Form Name via JavaScript; www.devasking.com. Retrieved July 11, 2022, from https://www.devasking.com/issue/get-form-name-via-javascript

Group, K. (2021, March 15). *7 Reasons Why VueJS Is So Popular | Kofi Group*. Kofi Group; www.kofi-group.com. https://www.kofi-group.com/7-reasons-why-vuejs-is-so-popular/

Gunjal, A. (2021, July 3). *Context API. The Context API can be used to share... | by Amol Gunjal | Medium*. Medium; amolbkgunjal.medium.com. https://amolbkgunjal.medium.com/context-api-ba403eed4c91

Handling Forms - vue.js. (n.d.). Handling Forms - Vue.Js; 012.vuejs.org. Retrieved July 11, 2022, from https://012.vuejs.org/guide/forms.html

Harrell, J. (2018, November 6). *Implicit state sharing: React's context API & provide/inject in Vue - LogRocket Blog*. LogRocket Blog; blog.logrocket. com. https://blog.logrocket.com/implicit-state-sharing-reacts-context-api-provide-inject-in-vue-679062a50f05/

How to add a Background Image in Vue.js | Reactgo. (n.d.). Reactgo; reactgo.com. Retrieved July 11, 2022, from https://reactgo.com/vue-background-image/

How to import and use image in a Vue single file component? (n.d.). NewbeDEV; newbedev.com. Retrieved July 11, 2022, from https://newbedev.com/how-to-import-and-use-image-in-a-vue-single-file-component

How to use routing in Vue.js to create a better user experience. (2018, June 28). freeCodeCamp.Org; www.freecodecamp.org. https://www.freecodecamp.org/news/how-to-use-routing-in-vue-js-to-create-a-better-user-experience-98d225bbcdd9/

https://nx-designs.ch/agile_downloads/public/Routing%20in%20vue.js.pdf

https://www.spaceo.ca/blog/vue-js-pros-and-cons/

Implementing Lazy Loading in Vue Apps. (2020, June 19). Implementing Lazy Loading in Vue Apps; academind.com. https://academind.com/tutorials/vue-lazy-loading

Implicit State Sharing in React & Vue | Jonathan Harrell. (n.d.). Implicit State Sharing in React & Vue | Jonathan Harrell; www.jonathan-harrell.com. Retrieved July 11, 2022, from https://www.jonathan-harrell.com/blog/implicit-state-sharing-in-react-vue/

intigriti. (2021, November 30). *Insecure Direct Object Reference (IDOR) - Intigriti*. Intigriti; blog.intigriti.com. https://blog.intigriti.com/hackademy/idor/

Intro | Testing Library. (2022, February 28). Intro | Testing Library; testing-library.com. https://testing-library.com/docs/vue-testing-library/intro/

JavaScript Form Validation. (n.d.). JavaScript Form Validation; www.w3schools.com. Retrieved July 11, 2022, from https://www.w3schools.com/JS//js_validation.asp

JavaScript Forms Validation. (n.d.). JavaScript Forms Validation; daks.me. Retrieved July 11, 2022, from https://daks.me/js_validation.php

JSX: The benefits of using it with Vue JS you should explore. (2020, July 17). Software Outsourcing Company; www.arrowhitech.com. https://www.arrowhitech.com/jsx-the-benefits-of-using-it-with-vue-js/

Khosravi, K. (2021, May 28). *Theming Vue.js with styled-components - LogRocket Blog*. LogRocket Blog; blog.logrocket.com. https://blog.logrocket.com/theming-vue-js-with-styled-components/

Kopachovets, O. (2021, July 22). *Vue.js Pros and Cons: Why to Choose It for Your App? | ProCoders*. ProCoders; procoders.tech. https://procoders.tech/blog/advantages-of-vue-js/

LaptrinhX. (2018, July 16). *Mocking HTTP requests with Nock | LaptrinhX*. Mocking HTTP Requests with Nock | LaptrinhX; laptrinhx.com. https://laptrinhx.com/mocking-http-requests-with-nock-2410543980/

LaptrinhX. (2021, February 4). *Styling a Vue.js application using CSS | LaptrinhX*. Styling a Vue.Js Application Using CSS | LaptrinhX; laptrinhx.com. https://laptrinhx.com/styling-a-vue-js-application-using-css-1604915263/

Lazy loading and code splitting in Vue.js – @tkssharma | Tarun Sharma | My Profile. (n.d.). Lazy Loading and Code Splitting in Vue.Js – @tkssharma | Tarun Sharma | My Profile; tkssharma.com. Retrieved July 11, 2022, from https://tkssharma.com/lazyloading-and-code-spitting-vuejs/

Lazy Loading Routes | Vue Router. (n.d.). Lazy Loading Routes | Vue Router; v3.router.vuejs.org. Retrieved July 11, 2022, from https://v3.router.vuejs.org/guide/advanced/lazy-loading.html

Lotanna, N. (2021, April 15). *Lazy loading components and code splitting in Vue.js - LogRocket Blog.* LogRocket Blog; blog.logrocket.com. https://blog.logrocket.com/vue-lazy-loading-components-code-splitting/

nock. (2022, July 1). *GitHub - nock/nock: HTTP server mocking and expectations library for Node.js.* GitHub; github.com. https://github.com/nock/nock

Oza, H. (n.d.). *The Demand to Hire Web Developers in 2022 – An In-Depth Insight into Web Development of the Future | Hyperlink InfoSystem.* The Demand to Hire Web Developers in 2022 – An In-Depth Insight into Web Development of the Future | Hyperlink InfoSystem; www.hyperlinkinfosystem.com. Retrieved July 11, 2022, from https://www.hyperlinkinfosystem.com/research/demand-to-hire-web-developers-in-2021

Programmatic Navigation | Vue Router. (n.d.). Programmatic Navigation | Vue Router; v3.router.vuejs.org. Retrieved July 11, 2022, from https://v3.router.vuejs.org/guide/essentials/navigation.html

Props | Vue.js. (n.d.). Props | Vue.Js; vuejs.org. Retrieved July 11, 2022, from https://vuejs.org/guide/components/props.html

r/node - We meme, but these kinds of job postings do exist! (7+ years of Vue experience when it hasn't existed that long?!) . (n.d.). Reddit; www.reddit.com. Retrieved July 11, 2022, from https://www.reddit.com/r/node/comments/sf5d29/we_meme_but_these_kinds_of_job_postings_do_exist/

React Context API - Why, How and When ? With full example. - DEV Community. (2021, August 16). DEV Community; dev.to. https://dev.to/ahmedm1999/react-context-api-why-how-and-when-with-full-example-28d0

React Context API: What is it and How it works? | LoginRadius Blog. (n.d.). React Context API: What Is It and How It Works? | LoginRadius Blog; www.loginradius.com. Retrieved July 11, 2022, from https://www.loginradius.com/blog/engineering/react-context-api/

Render Functions & JSX — Vue.js. (n.d.). Render Functions & JSX — Vue.Js; v2.vuejs.org. Retrieved July 11, 2022, from https://v2.vuejs.org/v2/guide/render-function?redirect=true

Sanchis, J. (2020, February 19). *Vue.js, the #1 powerful front-end development tool - Stratton Apps.* Stratton Apps; strattonapps.com. https://strattonapps.com/web-development/vuejs/vuejs-js-future-of-web/

shahbazchandio. (2020, July 21). *Routing – My Blog.* Routing – My Blog; computerprogramming.foobrdigital.com. https://computerprogramming.foobrdigital.com/routing/

Styling Vue components with CSS - Learn web development | MDN. (2022, May 23). Styling Vue Components with CSS - Learn Web Development | MDN; developer.mozilla.org. https://developer.mozilla.org/en-US/docs/Learn/Tools_and_testing/Client-side_JavaScript_frameworks/Vue_styling

Testing — Vue.js. (n.d.). Testing — Vue.Js; v2.vuejs.org. Retrieved July 11, 2022, from https://v2.vuejs.org/v2/guide/testing.html

Testing Vue Applications With The Vue Testing Library — Smashing Magazine. (2020, November 24). Smashing Magazine; www.smashingmagazine.com. https://www.smashingmagazine.com/2020/11/vue-applications-vue-testing-library/

The Pros and Cons of Vue.js | AltexSoft. (2019, September 11). AltexSoft; www.altexsoft.com. https://www.altexsoft.com/blog/engineering/pros-and-cons-of-vue-js/

Top 7 Useful JavaScript Open Source Framework - Corporate Today. (2020, July 12). Corporate Today; corporatetoday.org. https://corporatetoday.org/top-javascript-open-source-framework/

Understand React Context API. (2021, May 6). Telerik Blogs; www.telerik.com. https://www.telerik.com/blogs/understand-react-context-api

Using with Vuex | Vue Test Utils. (n.d.). Using with Vuex | Vue Test Utils; v1.test-utils.vuejs.org. Retrieved July 11, 2022, from https://v1.test-utils.vuejs.org/guides/using-with-vuex.html

v-if vs. v-show - Vue Conditional Rendering. (n.d.). V-If vs. v-Show - Vue Conditional Rendering; learnvue.co. Retrieved July 11, 2022, from https://learnvue.co/2021/05/v-if-vs-v-show-vue-conditional-rendering/

Vue | Best Vue development company in India. (2022, February 11). Pebery Technologies; peberytechnologies.com. https://peberytechnologies.com/technologies-vue/

Vue js – uilayouts. (n.d.). Vue Js – Uilayouts; uilayouts.com. Retrieved July 11, 2022, from https://uilayouts.com/category/vue-js/

vue js developed by. (2020, October 6). Humanity & Equality in Abortion Reform IOM; www.hearcampaign.im. http://www.hearcampaign.im/site/vue-js-developed-by-42326f

*Vue*コンテキスト引数の説明 — コンポジション*API*チュートリアル.(n.d.). ICHI.PRO; ichi.pro. Retrieved July 11, 2022, from https://ichi.pro/vue-kontekisuto-hikisu-no-setsumei-konpojishon-api-chu-toriaru-147676481601998

Vue.js - CodeDocs. (2019, July 1). Vue.Js - CodeDocs; codedocs.org. https://codedocs.org/what-is/vue-js

vue.js - When do you use the render function in vue? - Stack Overflow. (2020, June 23). Stack Overflow; stackoverflow.com. https://stackoverflow.com/questions/62527036/when-do-you-use-the-render-function-in-vue

Vue.js Conditional Rendering. (n.d.). Vue.Js Conditional Rendering; linuxhint.com. Retrieved July 11, 2022, from https://linuxhint.com/vue-js-conditional-rendering/

Vue.js Methods - GeeksforGeeks. (2020, September 13). GeeksforGeeks; www.geeksforgeeks.org. https://www.geeksforgeeks.org/vue-js-methods/

VueJS - Routing. (n.d.). VueJS - Routing; www.tutorialspoint.com. Retrieved July 11, 2022, from https://www.tutorialspoint.com/vuejs/vuejs_routing.htm

vuejs. (n.d.). *v2.vuejs.org/components-props.md at master · vuejs/v2.vuejs.org.* GitHub; github.com. Retrieved July 11, 2022, from https://github.com/vuejs/vuejs.org/blob/master/src/v2/guide/components-props.md

vuejs. (n.d.). *v2.vuejs.org/routing.md at master · vuejs/v2.vuejs.org*. GitHub; github. com. Retrieved July 11, 2022, from https://github.com/vuejs/vuejs.org/blob/ master/src/v2/guide/routing.md

yaoningvital. (2019, April 21). *Vue - Form Input Bindings · Issue #122 · yaoningvital/blog*. GitHub; github.com. https://github.com/yaoningvital/blog/ issues/122

Yoon, J.-Y. (2021, December 14). *Focal Adhesion | SpringerLink*. Focal Adhesion | SpringerLink; link.springer.com. https://link.springer.com/ chapter/10.1007/978-3-030-83696-2_7

Совместное использование Vue JSX: шаблон создания компонента, использование метода render и другие моменты. (2018, March 30). Совместное Использование Vue JSX: Шаблон Создания Компонента, Использование Метода Render и Другие Моменты; webformyself.com. https://webformyself.com/ispolzovanie-jsx-s-vue-i-zachem-eto-nuzhno/

Index

Printed in the United States
by Baker & Taylor Publisher Services